Adult Bible Study Series

by
Carl Roth

Written by Carl Roth

Edited by Rev. Peter Ledic and Pamela Nielsen

Scripture quotations are from The Holy Bible, English Standard Version®. Copyright © 2001 by Crossway Bibles, a publishing ministry of Good News Publishers, Wheaton, Illinois. Used by permission. All rights reserved.

Scripture quotations marked NIV are taken from the HOLY BIBLE, NEW INTERNATIONAL VERSION®. NIV®. Copyright © 1973, 1978, 1984 by International Bible Society. Used by permission of Zondervan Publishing House. All rights reserved.

Hymn texts and quotations with the abbreviation *LW* are from *Lutheran Worship*, copyright © 1982 Concordia Publishing House. All rights reserved.

Catechism quotations are from *Luther's Small Catechism with Explanation*, copyright © 1986, 1991 Concordia Publishing House.

The quotations from the Lutheran Confessions are from *Concordia: The Lutheran Confessions*, copyright © 2005 Concordia Publishing House. All rights reserved.

This publication may be available in braille, in large print, or on cassette tape for the visually impaired. Please allow 8 to 12 weeks for delivery. Write to the Library for the Blind, 7550 Watson Rd., St. Louis, MO 63119-4409; call toll-free 1-888-215-2455; or visit the Web site: www.blindmission.org.

Growing in Christ ® is published quarterly by Concordia Publishing House. Your comments and suggestions concerning this material are appreciated. E-mail us at sundayschool@cph.org.

Manufactured in the United States of America

Contents

Welcome to Growing in Christ!

Jesus says,

"Already you are clean because of the word that I have spoken to you. Abide in Me, and I in you. As the branch cannot bear fruit by itself, unless it abides in the vine, neither can you, unless you abide in Me. I am the vine; you are the branches." John 15:3–5

GROWING IN CHRIST is the life of the child of God! Through the Word and Sacraments, we live and grow in Christ.

GROWING IN CHRIST is a Sunday School curriculum rich in God's holy Word. Students learn all the major stories of the Old and New Testament and see how God weaves His plan of salvation in Christ through the lives of ordinary men, women, and children.

GROWING IN CHRIST puts the focus squarely on the heart and center of the entire Bible: Jesus Christ, our Savior from sin, death, and the devil. Each lesson reveals our sin and God's forgiving mercy in Christ.

GROWING IN CHRIST lessons connect the Word of God to the daily life of the student, nurturing faith in our loving, forgiving Savior.

GROWING IN CHRIST strengthens Christ-centered grateful response in lives marked by thanks and praise and service and obedience.

GROWING IN CHRIST teaches the language and shape of Christian faith and life in the Lutheran Church, grounding students in the Bible, Small Catechism, and hymnal.

GROWING IN CHRIST is the life of the child of God!

Introduction

God promises to strengthen our life in Christ as we study His Word. The Growing in Christ Bible Study series provides you resources to help you study God's Word. The series gives you an opportunity to study some familiar, and possibly not-so-familiar, biblical accounts in depth.

Each of the nine Bible study books has thirteen sessions that are divided into four easy-to-use sections.

Opening—Section 1 of each session points participants to the key point for the session and invites discussion and thinking to draw participants into the study.

God Speaks—Section 2 of each session explores a portion of Scripture through the use of a brief commentary and questions that help the participants study the text.

We Live—Section 3 of each session helps the participants apply to their lives both God's Law and Gospel revealed in the scriptural account.

Closing—Section 4 of each session provides the participants with practical suggestions for taking the theme of the lesson out of the classroom and into the world.

Growing in Christ is designed to assist both novice and expert Bible students in their study of Holy Scripture. It offers resources that will enable them to grow in their understanding of God's Word while strengthening their life in Christ.

As an added benefit, the sessions in the Growing in Christ Adult Bible Study series follow the Scripture lessons taught in the Growing in Christ Sunday School series. Parents will enjoy studying in depth the Bible stories their children are studying in Sunday School. This will provide parents and children additional opportunities to

- discuss God's Word together;
- extend lesson applications to everyday situations;
- pray together; and
- engage in family activities that grow out of lesson truths.

We encourage you to order the set of Bible Posters for this quarter. These large, beautifully rendered works of art will provide your class with memorable visuals of the texts they are studying. (To order, call 1-800-325-3040; ask for CPH stock number 44-1071.)

Adult Study Guide

World History	Dates	Biblical People
Egypt—Greco–Roman Period	332 BC	
Early Imperial China—Western Han	206 BC	
Roman Empire	63 BC	
Herod the Great	37 BC	
Augustus	27 BC	
	6 or 5 BC	Jesus born
India—Kushan Empire	AD 1	
	AD 5	Jesus in the temple at age 12
Agents from the Roman Empire begin rule	AD 6	
Early Imperial China—Hsing	AD 9	
Early Imperial China—Eastern Han	AD 25	
Pontius Pilate	AD 26	John the Baptizer begins ministry
	AD 27	Jesus baptized
	AD 29	Jesus transfigured
	AD 30	Jesus crucified

The Birth of John Foretold

Luke 1:5–25

Key Point

God in His mercy promised to send John to prepare sinful people for the coming of the Lord. God in His Word calls us to repentance, declaring us righteous because of Jesus.

Law/Gospel Points

Zechariah and Elizabeth were ordinary people, sinful just as I am. I need to repent and return to the Lord. **I, like them, stand righteous before God in spite of my sin, being justified by Christ, the Righteous One. God forgives me for Jesus' sake, drawing me to Him through His Word and Sacraments.**

God's Word (the Law) points out my sin and calls me to repentance. **God's Word proclaims forgiveness of sins and life in Christ for me.**

Connections

Bible Words

Repent therefore, and turn again, that your sins may be blotted out. Acts 3:19

Faith Words

Advent, prophecy, confession, absolution

Hymn

Arise, O Christian People (*LSB* 354; *TLH* 75)

Catechism

Lord's Prayer: Second Petition, Confession

Liturgy Link

Blue paraments

1 Opening

1. Today we begin the season of Advent. The word *advent* means "a coming to" or "an arrival." Today's lesson tells of the promise that John the Baptist would come to prepare the way for Jesus' own coming. In Advent, we focus on the advents (plural) of Jesus. Give three examples of advents of Jesus, and discuss how each one is important to our lives as Christians.

2. Today's lesson is set in and around the temple in Jerusalem. Though the inner workings of the temple, and the tabernacle before it, are unfamiliar to most of us, basic knowledge of them helps us understand many events and ideas in the New Testament. God's presence dwelled in the temple, and priests offered sacrifices to Him there, as He had instructed them to do. One of the rites of the temple was the burning of incense. Exodus 30:1–10 describes the institution of this rite. Zechariah was a priest, and he had been chosen to serve at the altar of incense, which was just outside the Holy of Holies (Luke 1:8–9). This was a once-in-a-lifetime opportunity and a high honor. While the priest offered incense, believers would offer prayers at the temple (Luke 1:10). What does incense symbolize? See Psalm 141:1–2. Why might God have instituted the use of incense for Old Testament worship?

3. God spoke to Zechariah through the angel Gabriel, the messenger whom He had sent. Angels were often sent by God to be His messengers. Who did Jesus later send out into the world as His messengers to speak on His behalf? Who are Jesus' messengers to the world today? How can we tell whether someone is a true or false messenger of God?

2 God Speaks

The Birth of John Foretold
Luke 1:5–25

Law

Our worldly understanding of righteousness is clouded by sin and human shortcomings. God alone knows and sees true righteousness. Although we might try for years to be righteous in word and deed like Zechariah, we would fall into sin at some point because all have sinned and fall short of the glory of God.

Gospel

If God were not merciful and gracious to us when we were yet sinners, we would be lost with no hope. Those who go forth with the Holy Spirit proclaim the fact that we have sinned and need a Savior.

Context

God set up the regulations for the tabernacle and later the temple in order to establish and maintain His people. God is merciful in providing sacrifices to cleanse that which is unclean and make holy that which is common.

Commentary

God promises to make His people a holy nation, a kingdom of priests. Zechariah followed all the temple regulations with the result that God's people were taught right from wrong and taught that God loves and forgives them.

The name *Zechariah* means "God will remember." God remembered His people by sending His holy messenger Gabriel to announce the birth of John, the forerunner and cousin of Jesus. Zechariah was not only rightfully gripped with fear, but he also doubted God's message.

Would we not also doubt? After all, God had not sent a prophet or an angel in centuries. Yet God forgave Zechariah's doubting and gave him the cross of muteness to bear as a sign of the coming blessing of John, whose name means "The Lord is gracious and moved to pity." The Scripture lessons appointed for this week speak blessing on those who receive the gracious Gospel message, but woe to those who reject it!

Even when we bear our crosses, they testify to Christ. In this world, He gives us so much joy that all suffering for His sake will be forgotten in heaven, swallowed up in His love and abundant gifts.

God knows us, loves us, and desires to save us even before we are born. God does not forgive us because of our worldly righteousness, but because Jesus exchanged His perfect righteousness for our deep and abiding sin when He was killed in our place on the cross. All those who speak the truth of

God's love speak about the person and work of Jesus for us. Our human thoughts and frailties do not limit God's love. Nothing is impossible with God.

Discussion questions

1. Luke 1:6 says that both Zechariah and Elizabeth were "righteous before God, walking blamelessly in all the commandments and statutes of the Lord." Why can this verse not mean that Zechariah and Elizabeth were saved by perfect obedience to the commandments? See Romans 3:23–24. What does it mean that they were "righteous before God"? What does it mean that they were "walking blamelessly" in God's commandments and statutes?

2. What Old Testament couple is brought to mind by the story of Zechariah and Elizabeth? See Genesis 17:15–19. What similarities do you see between the stories? Why is it important to read that the saints in the Bible sometimes fell into unbelief?

3. Malachi is the last book in the Old Testament and was written around 430 BC. Read Malachi 4:5–6 and Luke 1:16–17. What key phrases in these verses indicate that Malachi's prophecy was fulfilled in the person of John? What event does Malachi say will happen after Elijah comes?

4. Read Luke 3:3. What was John's basic message? According to Luke 1:16, what would be one outcome of John's preaching? If Luke 1:16 refers to the repentance of some of the Jews, to whom might Luke 1:17 be referring?

12

5. Luke 1:15 says that John "must not drink wine or strong drink." This is one of the requirements for someone who would take a Nazarite vow. Read Numbers 6:1–3. What is the purpose of the Nazarite vow? What kind of tone does this set for John's ministry? According to Psalm 104:15, what does wine symbolize? In Luke 7:33–34, Jesus contrasts His own ministry with John's, saying that John drinks no wine but that He does. What could this difference in their ministries indicate?

3 We Live

1. God made Zechariah mute because he did not believe the promise given through Gabriel. Zechariah would have known the story of Abraham and Sarah, among other similar stories, of God opening closed wombs. He should have known better than to doubt God. Instead, he asked for a sign to prove that the prophecy would come true. God muted Zechariah in order to chastise him for his unbelief but also, ironically, to provide the sign for which he had asked. When misfortunes occur in our lives, should we interpret them as God's punishments? Why or why not? What are the only signs of God's love for which we should look? Read Mark 16:16 and Romans 8:28. What are some examples of signs that people today seek in order to confirm that God loves them?

2. Luke 1:15 says that John would "be filled with the Holy Spirit, even from his mother's womb." Read Luke 1:39–45. Who alone can give faith? What could these passages tell us about the possibility of unborn babies having faith? Can we be certain that God gives faith to infants who are baptized? What impression do these passages give to us concerning the value Elizabeth and Mary placed on their unborn babies?

In ancient Israel, childlessness brought shame on women. After conceiving Joseph, Jacob's wife Rachel says, "God has taken away my reproach" (Genesis 30:23). In Luke 1:25, Elizabeth also speaks of having her reproach taken away. Childlessness was mistakenly thought to be a curse for sins committed. In other words, someone at the time of Zechariah and Elizabeth would have concluded that they had done something to cause God not to favor them with children. The actual reason that Zechariah and Elizabeth were unable to have a child was that Elizabeth was barren, and both of them were very old (Luke 1:7). Though they had continually prayed to God for a child (Luke 1:13), they had not received one. It is true that God is the only one who can open and close wombs (Genesis 30:22). Yet the fact that He had not blessed them with a child had not shaken their confidence in His love for them, as we know that they were "righteous before God" (Luke 1:6).

Even today, many couples struggle with infertility, and sometimes Christians conclude that the cause is that God is displeased with them. While it is true that children are always a great blessing, as Psalm 127:3–5 states, people who are unable to have children should never look at the absence of this blessing as a sign of God's disposition toward them. Childlessness is a difficult cross for couples to bear, but they can nonetheless count themselves blessed, since God "has blessed us in Christ with every spiritual blessing in the heavenly places" (Ephesians 1:3) and He promises that "all things work together for good, for those who are called according to his purpose" (Romans 8:28). If someone you know is struggling with infertility, include special petitions for them in your prayers this week. Pray that God would bless them with the gift of children if it is His will, but if it is not, that He would give them the strength to bear that cross faithfully.

4 Closing

Family Connections

Go over your child's Growing in Christ leaflet together, each of you sharing what you learned about today's Bible story.

One of the best things you can do for your family is to work on memorizing Luther's Small Catechism together. This week, our lesson discussed how John the Baptist would announce that the kingdom of God was at hand and call people to repentance. These topics are related to the Second Petition of the Lord's Prayer, "Thy kingdom come," and to Confession and Absolution in the Small Catechism. Luther reminds us that "God's kingdom comes when our heavenly Father gives us His Holy Spirit, so that by His grace we believe His holy Word and lead godly lives here in time and there in eternity." He also explains "Confession has two parts. First, that we confess our sins, and second, that we receive absolution, that is, forgiveness, from the pastor as from God Himself, not doubting, but firmly believing that by it our sins are forgiven before God in heaven." Review these sections of the Small Catechism in your family devotions this week and work on memorizing them.

Personal Reflection

After Elizabeth had conceived, "for five months she kept herself hidden, saying, 'Thus the Lord has done for me in the days when He looked on me, to take away my reproach among people'" (Luke 1:24–25). Why did Elizabeth go into seclusion? Based on what she says about the Lord's wonderful gift to her, perhaps the best explanation is that she wanted a period of time to devote herself to thanksgiving and prayer. She and Zechariah had prayed for a child for so long, and the Lord had finally answered their prayers with a "Yes!"

This week's lesson is full of references to prayer. Since Advent is a season of penitential preparation for the Lord's coming, it is a good time to focus on the daily discipline of prayer.

For Next Week

Now that we have learned of God's miraculous promise to provide a child to Zechariah and Elizabeth, next week we will study Gabriel's foretelling of Jesus' birth to Mary. Unlike Zechariah, Mary will receive Gabriel's message in faith and provide an example that we can all learn from: "Behold, I am the servant of the Lord; let it be to me according to your word" (Luke 1:38). To prepare for the next lesson, read the account of the annunciation in Luke 1:26–38. You may also want to look at Matthew 1:18–25, which provides further details about the child Jesus as they were revealed to Joseph in a dream.

The Birth of Jesus Foretold

Luke 1:26–38

Key Point

God favored Mary because of Christ, choosing her to be the mother of the Savior. God favors me because of Christ, choosing me to be His child.

Law/Gospel Points

Like Mary, I deserve nothing from God because of my sinfulness. **God grants me unmerited grace and favor because of His Son.**

God must punish sin. **In His mercy, God sends His Son to take my punishment upon Himself.**

Because of my sin I was separated from God. **Because of God's grace and favor, the Lord is with me.**

On my own, I am sinful and not blessed. **Christ blesses me with His presence, just as He did Mary and Elizabeth.**

Connections

Bible Words

Therefore the Lord Himself will give you a sign. Behold the virgin shall conceive and bear a son, and shall call His name Immanuel. Isaiah 7:14

Faith Words

crismon, annunciation, Messiah, Immanuel

Hymn

Jesus! Name of Wondrous Love (*LSB* 900; *LW* 182; *TLH* 114)

Catechism

Apostles' Creed: Second Article

1 Opening

1. Why is it absolutely essential that we maintain that Jesus was conceived without a human father while Mary was a virgin?

> 1. THE BIBLE SAYS SO
>
> 2. HUMAN PARENTS = ORIGINAL SIN

2. Gabriel says to Mary in Luke 1:37 that "Nothing will be impossible with God." How could this verse be misused by Christians today? How should we apply it?

> THEOLOGY OF GLORY
>
> GOD IS ABLE TO DO WHAT HE SAYS i.e. ex nihilo, REAL PRESENCE.

3. Is it appropriate to call Mary the mother of God?

> YES
>
> THE CONFESSIONS DO.

4. What is the traditional date for observation of the annunciation (Gabriel's announcement to Mary of Jesus' conception)? Does your congregation celebrate the annunciation?

> MARCH 25

2 God Speaks

The Birth of Jesus Foretold
Luke 1:26–38

Law
We, like Mary, are faced with the enormous pressure of bowing down to the way things appear to be. Our first instinct is to be wise in the ways of the world, which would make us fools before God.

Gospel
Neither Mary nor we chose God, but He chose Mary, and that same almighty God chooses us. Mary submitted to God's will because she first received the Gospel message of Jesus' birth. We submit to God's will and follow His commandments because we first received the Gospel.

Context

The angel Gabriel visited both Zechariah, the husband of Elizabeth, and Mary, Elizabeth's cousin. Elizabeth was too old to have a baby, while Mary was too young—still a virgin—and was only engaged to be married.

Commentary

While Elizabeth had the support of her husband, Mary faced the possible loss of her reputation, her family, her fiancé, and even her life. Not only could she be stoned to death for supposed adultery, but she could also die because of complications from pregnancy and childbirth. In spite of the looming mix of joy and fear at Gabriel's message, Mary passed the test. She does not question God but submits to His will because she first received the Gospel, the Christ to be born from her womb. Her faith accepted the unacceptable and, for Christ's sake, all generations do call her blessed.

As Paul says in Philippians and Luke says here, any good work or blessing comes through Jesus Christ alone, who will complete that good work in the day of His second coming, even as He will execute judgment on the wicked.

The Good News of Christ embraces both His suffering and death for us on Calvary and also His return as Lord and Judge. It is His Word that counts, not the words of the world. That means we can trust His Word in spite of all worldly cares and fears. We can accept the unacceptable in Christ's name.

Like Mary, we can bear the most fearful of crosses that God gives us as blessings in Christ. We believe that the worst evil that might strike us in this world cannot overcome the Judge of all worlds and ages.

Our victory in Christ is an eternal victory. Like Mary, we are eternally blessed.

Discussion questions

1. The angel Gabriel came to both Zechariah and Mary with prophecies of extraordinary births. Compare Zechariah's response in Luke 1:18 with Mary's responses in 1:34, 38. How are they different? What could account for the differences between their responses? What can we learn from this comparison?

2. In Luke 1:28, Mary is called "favored one," and in 1:30 she is told that she
has "found favor with God." What does *favor* mean? See Genesis 6:5–8 for
the first instance of the word *favor* in the Bible. What caused God to favor
Noah? What caused God to favor Mary? How does this shed light that we are
justified by grace?

GRACE

GRACE

3. Joshua was the successor of Moses and led the children of Israel
triumphantly into the Promised Land. His name means "the Lord helps" or
"the Lord saves." In a way, Joshua was a savior of Israel. *Jesus* is the Greek
form of the name *Joshua*. In Luke 1:31, Gabriel tells Mary that she will call
her son Jesus. How does Jesus' name reveal who He is? See Matthew 1:21.
How does Matthew define what kind of Savior Jesus is?

NOT AN EARTHLY KING COMING TO "SAVE" JUST
JEWS, BUT A SPIRITUAL KING TO SAVE
WHOLE WORLD

4. Read 2 Samuel 7:11b–16 and Isaiah 9:6–7. The first is a prophecy from the
Lord given through the prophet Nathan to King David that there would come
after him a King (Messiah or Christ) whose throne would endure forever. The
second is a prophecy from Isaiah concerning the Messiah. Compare these
prophecies to Luke 1:27, 32–33, 35, and note similar phrases. How does Luke
emphasize that Jesus will fulfill the Jewish hope for the long-awaited
Messiah? How does he reveal that Jesus is not a mere earthly king but is
actually God Himself?

3 We Live

1. The liturgy and confessions that we use in the Church help connect us historically to God's people of all times. Much of our liturgy is derived from the Psalms, the prayer book of the Old Testament. The Sanctus is from Isaiah 6, the Aaronic Benediction is from Numbers 6, and more Old Testament examples could be given. Of course, New Testament phrases and songs also appear in the liturgy. We also confess our faith through the Apostles' or Nicene Creeds, which declare what we believe about the God who created the world, redeemed us by the cross of Jesus, and sanctifies us through the Holy Spirit's continuing work. As we read the Old and New Testaments, we learn that they are truly part of the story of our lives as Christians. Christian doctrines are not just abstract statements disconnected from reality but are living descriptions of God's gracious dealings with His people of all times. We see an example of this in St. Mary. Where do we find her in our creeds and liturgy? How does the Church properly remember Mary?

RESPECTFULLY

2. In Luke 1:35, Gabriel says to Mary that "The Holy Spirit will come upon you, and the power of the Most High will overshadow you; therefore the child to be born will be called holy—the Son of God." Though Jesus is uniquely the Son of God, in what way can all Christians be called "holy" and "sons of God" through the work of the Holy Spirit? See 1 Corinthians 6:11; John 3:5; Galatians 3:26–27; Romans 8:14–17.

BAPTISM

3. A literal translation of Luke 1:28 from the Greek would be "Rejoice, favored woman, the Lord is with you." Gabriel indicates that the Lord's favor toward and presence with Mary are cause for rejoicing. In what unique sense was the Lord with Mary? See Matthew 1:23. Where do we find Immanuel today?

4 Closing

Family Connections

Go over your child's Growing in Christ leaflet together, each of you sharing what you learned about today's Bible story.

Perhaps Martin Luther's most beautiful confession of the Gospel is his explanation of the Second Article of the Apostles' Creed. This week is a particularly good time to review this part of the Small Catechism because of this lesson's promise of a Son to Mary. Luther places great emphasis on our Lord's incarnation (enfleshment) when he writes, "I believe that Jesus Christ, true God, begotten of the Father from eternity, and also true man, born of the Virgin Mary, is my Lord." For people seeking to find a gracious God, Luther would always point them to the Son of Mary. Review this section of the Small Catechism in your family devotions this week and work on memorizing it.

Personal Reflection

"Our churches teach that the history of saints may be set before us so that we may follow the example of their faith and good works, according to our calling" (AC XXI 1). Lutherans always have honored the saints who have passed before them into glory. We remember them with thanksgiving in order that their example would be an encouragement for our lives. Out of joy over the child in her womb, St. Mary sang, "For behold, from now on all generations will call me blessed; for He who is mighty has done great things for me, and holy is His name" (Luke 1:48–49). She knew firsthand how wonderful the works of the Lord are. We do not call Mary blessed because of her own piety or good works, but because of the mighty realities that the Lord achieved through her.

We can learn much from this "highly favored mother." Her glorious hymn of praise, the Magnificat (Luke 1:46–55), puts into practice the words of the Psalmist: "I will bless the LORD at all times; His praise shall continually be in my mouth" (Psalm 34:1). Martin Luther suggested that everyone should learn the Magnificat by heart. This hymn is not just Mary's hymn but ours too. The Magnificat sings the praise of the God who created the world out of nothing and who creates faith and life in sinners who have nothing but death in themselves. It is a glorious confession that the Creator remembered His promises to Israel and still remembers them today. We are blessed, for the Savior whom Mary once held in her arms holds us up with His mighty arms. He remembers His mercy to us by daily sustaining our lives and faith.

The Mighty One has done great things for us, and His name is holy. Consider including the Magnificat in your daily prayers this week as a reminder of God's wonderful mercy shown to us through the child of St. Mary.

For Next Week

Last week, we studied Luke 1:5–25 and learned of the promise to Zechariah and Elizabeth that they would have a son named John. This week, we learned in Luke 1:26–38 that Mary also would have a son. Next week, we will see the promise to Zechariah and Elizabeth fulfilled in Luke 1:57–80. Read this section in preparation for class, and pay particular attention to 1:67–79, which is Zechariah's profound hymn of praise to God for His faithful remembrance of His people.

The Birth of John

Luke 1:57–80

Key Point

Zechariah spoke God's Word announcing that John would give people knowledge of salvation in the forgiveness of sins. God speaks through His holy Word to give me knowledge of salvation and forgiveness through Jesus, His Son.

Law/Gospel Points

God wants me to listen and obey Him, following His ways. **God looks at me through the obedience of Christ and is pleased.**

The world, including me, was lost in the darkness of sin and death. **God gives the world His Word, which proclaims forgiveness of sins and life and light in Christ Jesus.**

Because of my sin, I doubt and fear and need to hear God's words of forgiveness, life, and salvation. **God provides me with pastors who preach the Good News of Jesus.**

Connections

Bible words

Behold, the Lamb of God, who takes away the sin of the world! John 1:29

Faith Words

forgiveness, holiness, mercy, prophet

Hymn

Comfort, Comfort These My People (*LSB* 347; *LW* 28; *TLH* 61)

Catechism

Apostles' Creed: Third Article; Baptism; Confession and Absolution—Office of the Keys; Lord's Prayer: Conclusion; Sacrament of the Altar

Liturgy Link

The Introit

1 Opening

1. Have you ever been told that you have to learn to forgive yourself when you feel guilty about something? As a Christian, what is the problem with that statement? Read Psalm 51:1–5. What might David tell us to say instead of "You have to learn to forgive yourself"?

2. In the ancient world, names carried much more meaning than they do in our culture. We say in the Lord's Prayer that God's name is holy by saying "Hallowed be Thy name." Last week, we learned that Jesus' name is significant because it means "the Lord saves," and Jesus was born to save His people from their sins. Luke 1:13 says that Gabriel instructed Zechariah to name his son John, which means, "The Lord is gracious and moved to pity." We see in Luke 1:59 that the neighbors and family of Zechariah and Elizabeth expected the boy to be named after his father. How was the name *John* appropriate for his mission? What is the significance of having the name of God placed upon us in Baptism? See Matthew 28:19.

2 God Speaks

The Birth of John
Luke 1:57–80

Law

Even the best and most pious people of this world cannot measure up to God's standard for perfection. We all face turning points in our lives. Without God's Word, we cannot please God with our choices. Like Zechariah, we are faced with pressure to choose a path that leads away from God.

Gospel

This world is passing away, but the Word of the Lord and the kingdom of God endure forever. Through our Baptism, Christ gives us His righteousness and perfection, which surpass all earthly excellence.

24

Context

With friends and relatives gathered on the eighth day after the birth of their son, Zechariah proclaims his name to be John. His startling announcement and restored voice allow Zechariah to prophesy concerning his son's future ministry.

Commentary

Elizabeth and Zechariah were both of pure Levite ancestry, as was Mary. They were both pious and observant of the Torah, the instruction concerning the commands and blessings of the Lord. Their son was born, the greatest of all earthly Levites, surpassing even Aaron (and second only to his cousin Jesus), although the Christian priesthood shared by all believers would be greater still (Matthew 11:11–15). Zechariah's relatives had their own plans, which were different than God's. So Zechariah faced a fork in the road. Being devoted to God's Word along with his wife, he followed that Word and fulfilled the prophecy by naming his son John. As a result, God lifted the cross of muteness, and Zechariah prophesied concerning his son and the Christ who would follow.

We have no alternative than to go back to the basics, to our baptismal identity and the Word of God, when faced with a serious fork in the road in order to keep walking in God's light.

God's Word comforts us when we go to it as the wellspring of faith. God's Word strengthens us when we falter. As with Zechariah, it guides us when the turning point to or away from God is at hand. As with Zechariah, it gives us the hindsight to see our past trials as true blessings that have built us up in faith.

The Lord is near; rejoice! You, who have been made to walk in His light, praise Him. Your deliverance is at hand.

Discussion questions

Zechariah's prophecy in Luke 1:68–79 introduces many themes that will recur throughout Luke's Gospel. In the God Speaks and We Live sections, we will discuss seven important words that Luke uses: *covenant, prophet, forgiveness, righteousness, holiness, mercy,* and *peace.*

1. When would you hear the word *covenant* used today outside of biblical usage? Read Luke 1:68, 72–73. When these verses are connected, they show Zechariah saying, "Blessed be the Lord God of Israel, for He has visited and redeemed His people . . . to show the mercy promised to our fathers and to remember His holy covenant, the oath that He swore to our father Abraham." God made many covenants with His people and always swore to be faithful to them. The central thought of Zechariah's prophecy is that God remembers His

covenants. The covenant referred to here is the one God made with Abraham in Genesis 15; the oath is found in Genesis 22:15–18. All of the covenants God made with Israel were fulfilled in the Messiah, Jesus. Read Jeremiah 31:31–34. What did God promise to do here? Read Luke 22:20. How does Jesus show that we live under the new covenant?

2. The Old Testament prophets had many roles. They encouraged the people to rely on the Lord's strength and not their own. They called on the people to remember God's covenants with them. They proclaimed the Lord's faithfulness based on the saving acts He had performed in the past. And they prophesied what the Lord would do for His people in the future. All of these prophetic functions are included in Zechariah's prophecy in Luke 1:68–79. He was filled with the Holy Spirit, who allowed Him to prophesy (Luke 1:67). What would his son, John, do as a prophet (Luke 1:76–77)? Who would John prophesy about (Luke 1:78–79)? Who else had prophesied concerning John (Luke 3:4)? Who was the last and greatest of the prophets (Luke 4:24)?

3. Psalm 51 shows us that sin is what separates us from God. "Against You, You only, have I sinned and done what is evil in Your sight" (Psalm 51:4). The forgiveness of sins is emphasized in Luke and in the Bible in general. Luke tells us that salvation is found in the forgiveness of sins (Luke 1:77). John the Baptist identifies Jesus as "the Lamb of God, who takes away the sin of the world" (John 1:29). How would John the Baptist deliver forgiveness to people (Luke 3:3)? What does Jesus identify as the essential message of the Christian Church (Luke 24:47)? What is the basis for that message (Luke 24:46)? Why is this message so important?

4. A word closely related to the forgiveness of sins is *righteousness*. Zechariah says in Luke 1:74–75 that the Lord granted His people "to serve Him without fear, in holiness and righteousness before Him all our days." Read Romans 4:1–9 and Luke 18:9–14. What does the word *justify* mean? What does it mean that God "justifies the ungodly" (Romans 4:5)? In Luke 1:6 and 2:25, Zechariah, Elizabeth, and Simeon are described as "righteous." Why are they called righteous? How are people justified?

3 We Live

1. People are insultingly called "holier than thou" when they flaunt their piety and good works before others and condemn behaviors that they consider unholy. The temperance movement of the late nineteenth and early twentieth centuries was a holiness movement intended to make the production and use of alcohol illegal. Holiness churches require their members to abstain from things that they consider unholy, such as alcohol, tobacco, caffeine, and so on. What understanding of the word *holy* do we get based on the examples above? Read Luke 1:49, 70, 72, 75; 3:16. What do we learn about holiness from these passages? List as many things as you can that go on in Lutheran churches that we call holy. What makes these things holy?

2. What is mercy? See Luke 1:50, 54, 58, 72, 77–78; 6:36; 10:37. What do we learn about God's mercy from these verses? What do we learn about the mercy that we are to show to others?

3. What is your idea of perfect peace? Luke 1:79 says that Jesus will "guide our feet into the way of peace." In 2:14, we are told that Jesus' birth has brought "on earth peace among those with whom He is pleased!" Read Luke 2:29–30. How was peace brought to Simeon? Read Luke 24:36–39. How does Jesus show His disciples true peace?

4. In Luke 1:57–66, we see the neighbors and relatives of Zechariah and Elizabeth playing an important role in the circumcision and naming of John. Close relationships with extended families and tight connections with the community were the norm at this time. Many people never traveled more than a couple days' journey from where they grew up. This is hard for us to understand. While we can be thankful for the blessings of increased mobility in our times, we also should recognize the consequences, such as the disconnection of most of our lives from extended family and neighbors. Many people feel isolated and that their lives are fragmented and chaotic with no solid foundations anywhere. Since Christian congregations are made up of sons and daughters of God who are brothers and sisters in Christ, what responsibilities and opportunities are presented to the Church by our cultural climate?

4 Closing

Family Connections

Go over your child's Growing in Christ leaflet together, each of you sharing what you learned about today's Bible story.

Luke uses a vivid metaphor of the Lord's strength when he says that He "has raised up a horn of salvation for us in the house of His servant David" (1:69). Often the word *horn* is used in the Old Testament to describe God's power. Like a bull's horns, the horn of salvation, or God's Messiah, would have great strength. Try explaining this expression to your children, as they should be able to relate it to what they know about certain animals.

This week's lesson emphasized that John would "give knowledge of salvation to His people in the forgiveness of their sins" (Luke 1:77). The Small Catechism also places much emphasis on the forgiveness of sins. In Luther's explanation to the Third Article of the Creed, he says that the Holy Spirit "daily and richly forgives all my sins and the sins of all believers" in the Christian Church. Holy Baptism "works forgiveness of sins, rescues from death and the devil, and gives eternal salvation to all who believe this, as the words and promises of God declare." In Holy Absolution, "we receive absolution, that is, forgiveness, from the pastor as from God Himself, not doubting, but firmly believing that by it our sins are forgiven before God in heaven." In Holy Communion, Christ's body and blood give us "forgiveness of sins, life, and salvation."

In your family devotions, emphasize the forgiveness of sins that God gives us through Word and Sacrament. Review and work on memorizing the parts of the Small Catechism that deal with forgiveness. And remember to discuss the importance of forgiving each other, recalling these words from the Lord's Prayer: "as we forgive those who trespass against us."

Personal Reflection

Luke 1:68–79 is often called the Benedictus, a Latin word for *blessed*, the first word of the canticle. Almost every verse has a direct parallel in the Old Testament. This mighty hymn of God's salvation is often sung during the liturgies of Matins and Morning Prayer in our Lutheran hymnals. As you prepare for the celebration of the Lord's incarnation next week, consider praying or singing the Benedictus during your devotions. As Zechariah prophesied of Jesus, "the sunrise shall visit us from on high to give light to those who sit in darkness and in the shadow of death, to guide our feet into the way of peace" (Luke 1:78–79). In the midst of the darkness and cold that many of us experience during this winter season, the rays of the Son, the light of the world, break through our gloom.

For Next Week

It's almost here! By now our anticipation of Christmas has reached a fevered pitch. We are caught up with preparations, presents, parties, vacation from work and school, and travel. But let's not forget about the greater reality of Christmas, which is the incarnation of the Son of God. Finding ourselves at church on Christmas Eve and Christmas Day will help us stay tuned into this great story. And daily devotions will help too. In preparation for next week's lesson, read Luke 2:1–20, the account of Jesus' birth. Also read John 1:1–18 for a different but complementary look at the incarnation.

The Birth of Jesus

Luke 2:1–20

Key Point

A Savior has been born to you. He is Christ the Lord.

Law/Gospel Points

Because of my sin, I fear God as the shepherds did. **God's Son, Jesus, takes away my fear and offers me true peace.**

Because of sin, I am helpless before God and deserve to die. **God sent His Son, Jesus, to save me from sin and death.**

Connections

Bible Words

For God so loved the world, that He gave His only Son, that whoever believes in Him should not perish but have eternal life. John 3:16

Faith Words

census, Christ, Savior, peace

Hymn

Infant Holy, Infant Lowly (*LSB* 393; *HS98* 812)
God Loved the World So that He Gave (*LSB* 571; *LW* 352; *TLH* 245)

Catechism

Apostles' Creed: Second Article

Liturgy Link

Gloria in Excelsis

1 Opening

In the Roman Catholic Church, the order of service with the Lord's Supper was—and still is today—called the Mass. Therefore, the Mass on the celebration of Christ's birth came to be known as Christ's Mass in English, which was shortened to Christmas. At the time of the Reformation, Lutheran churches still called Communion services Mass. "The Mass is held among us and celebrated with the highest reverence" (AC XXIV 1). Yet because of the false Roman Catholic doctrine that in the Mass the priest offers up the body and blood of Christ as a sacrifice for the sins of the people, which turns the Lord's Supper into a work rather than a gift, most Lutherans have chosen not to continue using the term *Mass* (though it is just fine if they do). Today, many refer to the Communion service as the Divine Service, that is, God's gracious service to us in Word and Sacrament. But since Mass is part of the word *Christmas*, it reminds us that, historically speaking, the Lord's Supper was always celebrated on Christmas Day.

1. Why is Christmas a particularly fitting time to celebrate the Lord's Supper?

2. Around this time of year, you often see the phrase "Jesus is the reason for the season" on church signs and billboards. Read Luke 2:10–11. Who does the angel say is the reason for the season? Read John 1:1–4. How do we know that Jesus does not need a season for His own sake?

3. "Christmas is for children," people often say. Usually they mean that the excitement of music and presents and Santa Claus is particularly for little children. Read John 1:12–14. How is it that, in a very real and positive sense, Christmas is for children? In what negative way are all of us too often children at Christmas?

4. When you hear that something is a story, do you think first of fiction or non-fiction? When discussing the Christmas story and Bible stories with others, how can we best communicate that they are not just made-up?

2 God Speaks

The Birth of Jesus
Luke 2:1–20

Law
Without a Savior, we would have no hope. We would fall into despair, call on the mountains to cover us (Hosea 10:8; Luke 23:30), seek our own demise, and find only the terrible, divine Judge who would condemn us to an eternity of suffering.

Gospel
In the despair of our sin, God in His mercy reveals our salvation as Christ Jesus takes on human flesh. Jesus' birth, like His resurrection, points us heavenward to the rejoicing over God's redeeming His creation so that it would not be lost forever in sin but would endure forever with Him.

Context
Luke makes sure to proclaim Jesus as a real man born in the historical events of this world. The story of Jesus is not a moralizing fable.

Commentary
The story of Jesus' birth is a real event. In the text, we see His mother, Mary, plodding along a dusty road with the discomforts of a woman in her third trimester. She is great with child. We can only imagine the writhing agony of childbirth. We see the suckling Jesus wrapped in cloths and lying in a hay-filled feeding trough. We see otherwise nameless shepherds praising this newborn as the Savior of God's people. We see parents caught up in the drama that includes birth, blood, and humility as well as the rejoicing of the heavenly armies.

Heaven and earth meet in this baby, the swaddled Lord of all creation nursing at His mother's breast. We hear in the Scriptures how the Lord set aside His greatness to become humble. Yet through His humility, He makes the humble great and seats common folk among the greatest of the heavenly powers.

When God catches us up in His plans, we simply receive the words and works He would have us do, and like Mary, we ponder the greatness of our merciful Lord in our hearts.

We confess that the bloody birth and death of Jesus lead us to the empty tomb and the heavenly throne, where our Lord's wounds are badges of everlasting honor and His earthly grief becomes His—and our—eternal glory. "Worthy is the Lamb, who was slain" (Revelation 5:12).

Discussion questions

1. We should thank God for the remarkable literary and historical skills that St. Luke received from Him. In his Gospel, Luke eloquently and accurately portrays Jesus as a real man born within an actual historical context. How do we know that Luke was careful to keep his facts straight? Read Luke 1:1–4. What statements in Luke 2:1–2 provide the historical setting for this factual account? Why do you think Luke sets Jesus' birth on the stage of well-known world history?

2. King David was from Bethlehem and was a shepherd (1 Samuel 16:1, 11). We saw in Lesson 2 that the promised Messiah (also known as the Christ or Anointed One) would come from David's household (2 Samuel 7:12–16). Why was it necessary that Jesus be born in Bethlehem? See Micah 5:2–5a. What group of persons are mentioned in Luke 2:8–20 that are such fitting candidates to receive the Good News about the Messiah?

3. Luke 2:11 says that the child who is born in Bethlehem is Christ the Lord. We know from previous questions and lessons that the Messiah (the Christ) would be a successor to King David and would be very great. What did people commonly expect the Messiah to be like? See Luke 23:35, 39; Matthew 16:15–23; Acts 1:6. Where could they have looked for a correct understanding of what the Messiah would be like? See Isaiah 52:13–53:12.

4. Isaiah 52–53 describes the Lord's Suffering Servant in remarkable detail. Why would we talk about this passage on Christmas when it seems more appropriate for Good Friday? It helps us remember that Jesus was born to die. His death was foreseen in Scripture, as Jesus Himself teaches the disciples in Luke 24:25–27, 44–47. Isaiah 52–53 is just one instance of prophecy that the Christ would suffer, die, and rise again. As Luke says, "[Jesus] interpreted to them in all the Scriptures the things concerning Himself" (Luke 24:27). One of the passages we are studying in this lesson is John 3:16, "For God so loved the world, that He gave His only Son that whoever believes in Him should not perish but have eternal life." In light of the things we have learned about the Messiah, what do you think is the best interpretation of the phrases "God so loved the world" and "He gave His only Son"?

3 We Live

1. Read Luke 2:6–7. Perhaps the best word to describe the circumstances surrounding Jesus' birth is *humble*. There is nothing impressive about the birth itself. Only a few people knew about it. The glory of it is only shown through the angels, the messengers of God. The same can be said of the Church. She is not very impressive in the eyes of the world. The glory of the Church is only seen through the message of the Gospel given through the Word. Only the eyes of faith can see her glory. Christ's birth, life, and death reveal God's way of working in the world. We can also see that way of working in Christ's bride, the Church. Read Luke 1:48, 52; 14:7–11. How important is humility for the Christian? How does that virtue work itself out in practice?

2. At Christmas, we celebrate the wonderful truth that God took on human flesh in the womb of the Virgin Mary. The Creator of the universe made Himself into a tiny unborn baby. Though this is a time of year for joy and peace, the harsh reality of this sinful world is that many unborn babies are not safe in their mothers' wombs but will be murdered through abortion. As we remember our Lord's incarnation, let us reflect on the great tragedy and

injustice of abortion and seek ways to protect the little ones. The incarnation is the ultimate testament to the great value of unborn babies and little children. We also should remember that Jesus came to save sinners, including those who have had and perform abortions. What was Jesus' attitude toward infants? Read Luke 18:15–17. Why must we adults constantly learn to be children?

3. The angel in Luke 2:11 announced that a Savior had been born. Many Jews thought that the Messiah would be a secular savior who would defeat their enemies. What kind of savior are people looking for today? What kind of Savior is Jesus? See Matthew 1:21; Luke 1:77.

4. Don't the nativity scenes make you wish you were there? Don't the Christmas carols paint such a lovely picture of that night when Christ the Lord was born? Can you imagine how beautiful the angels' song was? It certainly would have been a glorious experience. But we have things even better than the shepherds. How?

4 Closing

Family Connections

Go over your child's Growing in Christ leaflet together, each of you sharing what you learned about today's Bible story.

Luther's explanation of the Second Article of the Creed in the Small Catechism gives a wonderful summary of why Jesus became man. Recite the Second Article and its Explanation at family devotions this week, since it truly shows the reason for the season.

Personal Reflection

The Christmas story is for you. You once were lowly, naked, ashamed, and afraid, entangled in sin. The Lord came as a naked newborn on a mission to wash you and cover you with the spotless robe of His righteousness. The wood of His manger foreshadowed the wood of His cross. The hymn "What Child Is This" emphasizes the reason for Jesus' incarnation: "Nails, spear shall pierce Him through, The cross be borne for me, for you" (LW 61:2). Through His sinless life, atoning death, and glorious resurrection, you now have life. Christmas is about God coming to you. The reason for the Christmas season is that you may come to receive gifts from the incarnate Savior of the world. These are imperishable gifts—the forgiveness of sins, life, and salvation—that are found in humble, fleshly sacramental signs. They are words, water, bread and wine, which bring peace and show God's good will toward you. This week, in your personal devotions, reflect on the fact that Christ is still present with you in Word and Sacrament. Thank Him for His presence and pray that He would continue to be our Immanuel, "God with us."

For Next Week

"For we do not have a high priest who is unable to sympathize with our weaknesses, but One who in every respect has been tempted as we are, yet without sin" (Hebrews 4:15). Our true High Priest, Jesus, had a typical childhood. He had to obey His parents, do chores, and go to bed at a certain time. He was tempted to disobey, but He never gave in to those temptations. He resisted every temptation without sinning in order to fulfill the Law's demands for perfect obedience. He did what we could never do! Though it is hard to imagine why this God-man would need to increase "in wisdom and in stature and in favor with God and man" (Luke 2:52), He did. Next week, we will continue to celebrate our Lord's incarnation by studying the only recorded story of Jesus' later childhood. He shows that He knows who His Father is through His desire to spend time in His Father's house, the Jerusalem temple. Read Luke 2:41–52 in preparation for next week's lesson.

The Boy Jesus in the Temple

Luke 2:41–52

Key Point

As a boy, Jesus was found in His Father's house. In God's house, I hear His Word, see that Jesus is my Savior, and receive His gifts of forgiveness and salvation.

Law/Gospel Points

Because of sin, I, like Jesus' parents, do not understand what God says to me. **God makes His Word clear to me through the power of the Holy Spirit.**

Because of my sin, I need a Savior. **God sent His Son to be my Savior.**

Because of sin, I cannot recognize who Jesus is. **Through Baptism and the power of God's Word, God makes clear to me that Jesus is God's Son and my Savior.**

Connections

Bible Words
O LORD, I love the habitation of Your house and the place where Your glory dwells. Psalm 26:8

Faith Words
Sabbath, faith, Word, means of grace

Hymn
The Gifts Christ Freely Gives (*LSB* 602)

Catechism
Third and Fourth Commandments

1 Opening

1. Why do you think that Luke 2:41–52 is the only account we have of Jesus' words and deeds between His infancy and adulthood? See John 20:30–31; 21:25.

2. Studying our Lord's childhood at Christmas reminds us of the truly ordinary and human aspects of His life. Of course, the visit from Gabriel and the shepherds was quite exceptional, but otherwise the experience of Mary and Joseph was not so different from that of any first-time parents. We are told that Mary treasured all these things in her heart (Luke 2:19, 51). Like any mother, she cherished the memories of her child's early days. But what else could Mary's careful remembrance of all of these events suggest? See Luke 1:1–4.

3. Jerusalem plays a major role in Luke's Gospel. In fact, Luke can be read as a description of Jesus' journey to, from, and around the city as He works toward accomplishing His mission. We see in Luke 2:22 that Jesus was presented at the temple in Jerusalem at the age of forty days. Luke 2:41 tells us that Jesus' family went annually to Jerusalem to celebrate the Passover. Why was Jerusalem such an important place? For what would Jesus eventually journey up to Jerusalem? See Luke 18:31–34. How would Jerusalem factor into the mission of the early Christian community? See Luke 24:46–49. As Christians, where is our true Jerusalem? See Hebrews 12:22–24.

2 God Speaks

The Boy Jesus in the Temple
Luke 2:41–52

Law
Because of sin, I, like Jesus' parents, do not understand what God says to me.

Gospel
The boy Jesus reveals His true identity and purpose as the Lamb of God. God makes His Word clear to me through the power of the Holy Spirit.

Context
The Christmas season continues with this account of the childhood of Jesus. This passage contains the last of the three scenes in the infancy narrative of Jesus in Luke 2: His birth, His presentation at His temple, and His return to His temple.

Commentary
Jesus and His parents, Mary and Joseph, travel to Jerusalem for the Feast of Passover. Jerusalem is on a high point geographically, but it was also the center of the Jewish religion. People then talked about going up to Jerusalem as British students today talk about going up to Oxford.

As pious Jews, Mary and Joseph did this often. But this time something special happened: Jesus uttered His first recorded words. In doing so, Jesus revealed His true identity and purpose. He is the Lamb of God who takes away the sins of the world. At Passover, the paschal lamb was slain at the temple. How filled with meaning is this account of the true and final Lamb of God coming to worship at the temple!

After Passover, the family began the journey back home, traveling in a caravan to provide one another with mutual aid and protection since bands of robbers would hide along the roads and assault unprotected travelers. Hence it was not unusual for Mary and Joseph to assume early in the return trip that Jesus was running around with His friends and would eventually show up. When He didn't, they became concerned and went back to Jerusalem to hunt for Him. Imagine their anxiety! Finally, they found Him in the temple.

To their astonishment, they found their young son carrying on a learned discussion with the Bible scholars (KJV: "doctors"). They admonish Him, as one would expect. But He gives a profound answer, "Why were you looking for Me? Did you not know that I must be in My Father's house?" (Luke 2:49). The text goes on to say that they did not understand what Jesus had said to them. Had they known His true identity, they would have gone straight to the temple to find Him instead of looking around Jerusalem for three days.

We are like Mary and Joseph. We understand very little of God's Word. We are slow to comprehend, and our hearts resist divine revelation. Yet despite our faults, we have a gracious God who comes to us in the person of His Son—yes, even His twelve-year-old Son—Jesus Christ. Jesus is teaching His parents—and us—that He *is* the temple that will be destroyed and yet rebuilt in three days. He is right where He should be. He is about the things (KJV: "business") of His Father. Who is His true Father? God Almighty. And what is that business? That He would go to the cross and die for our sins and on the third day rise again, giving us the forgiveness of sins and everlasting life. The phrase "it is necessary," or "must," is often used in connection with the Passion of Christ. The same Greek word is used in Luke 24:7: "The Son of Man must be delivered into the hands of sinful men and be crucified and on the third day rise." The Passion of the Lamb of God purchases salvation for us.

Discussion questions

1. Mary and Joseph went every year to the Feast of the Passover in Jerusalem (Luke 2:41). The institution of the Passover is recorded in Exodus 12. God was going to inflict His final plague on Egypt, the death of every firstborn male. But for the children of Israel, the angel of death would pass over every house that had a sacrificed lamb's blood on its lintel and doorframes. This final plague opened the door for Israel's exodus from Egyptian slavery. Every year, the children of Israel would celebrate the Passover, recalling God's salvation of Israel. Part of the celebration involved the sacrificing of a lamb and then a family meal consisting of that lamb and unleavened bread. The fact that Jesus was present in Jerusalem as a child for this feast is significant. The only other time in Luke's Gospel when the Passover is mentioned is in chapter 22, the account of the Last Supper. Read Luke 22:7–20 and John 1:29. How are the Passover Feast and the Lord's Supper related?

2. How does Luke show in this lesson that Jesus is the Son of God? Where else does he teach this doctrine? See Luke 1:35; 10:22; 22:29; and 24:49. As the Son of God, is Jesus less God than the Father? Why or why not?

3. We have seen above how Luke shows that Jesus is true God. His true humanity is also seen in this lesson. Where do we see that Jesus grew and developed just as any other child? How is His development possible, since as God He is omniscient and omnipotent? See Philippians 2:5–8 and Hebrews 5:8.

4. Mary and Joseph had both been visited by Gabriel concerning Jesus' miraculous birth and had heard amazing things about Him from the shepherds and Simeon. Yet they expressed astonishment at the knowledge He displayed in the temple (Luke 2:48) and did not understand His answer to their questions (Luke 2:50). Why might they have been so confused about His knowledge of God and His reference to being in His Father's house? See Mark 3:20–21. Who else often misunderstood Jesus' words? See Luke 9:44–45; 18:31–34.

5. Luke 2:49 says that Jesus asked His parents, "Did you not know that I must be in my Father's house?" The word *must* indicates necessity. There was simply no other way for Jesus to act than to seek out His Father's house. What other part of His mission had the same sense of necessity? See Luke 4:43; 9:22; 17:25.

3 We Live

1. In today's lesson, Jesus goes to the temple at age 12. We learn that He was asking and answering questions about the Old Testament. Jews considered twelve to be the age of religious maturity. Though there is no direct correlation, it is interesting that many Lutheran churches enroll students in confirmation classes around this age. Why is confirmation important? Is the rite absolutely necessary? How can we help children and adults who are going through confirmation classes?

2. Did Jesus sin by remaining in Jerusalem and not going back to Nazareth with His parents? No! Hebrews 4:15 tells us that Jesus was like us in every way except for sin, so it would be impossible to interpret this as disobedience. Even though Mary chastised Him, He had done nothing wrong. If anything, His duty to be in His Father's house was a higher one for, as Peter says, "We must obey God rather than men" (Acts 5:29) when there is a conflict between God's will and the will of humans. In any case, Jesus was patient with His parents. They did not understand His words (Luke 2:50). He provided a model for all children by submitting Himself to His parents (Luke 2:51). As one version of the hymn "Once in Royal David's City" says, "Christian children all must be mild, obedient, good as He." Of course, we have to acknowledge that as sinners our children will never achieve such a high standard. But while Jesus is foremost our Savior from sin, He is also our example for living the Christian life. This does not mean we need to continually ask the question, "What would Jesus do?" Actually, we can never know exactly what Jesus would do in a specific situation. The better question is, "What has Jesus already done and is still doing to save me?" Read Matthew 20:25–28. How does Jesus show that He is both the Savior of all people and their example?

3. The temple in Jerusalem was not simply a religious building. The most common name for the temple in the Bible is the house of the Lord. This shows that it was understood as the residence of God, where sacrifices could be made to Him. It was not simply a place of public worship and prayer. Actually, the general public could only go in the temple courts and not to its innermost parts. In fact, the priests of the temple could not just wander about anywhere inside. Only the chief priest could go into the Holy of Holies, and that was only once a year on the Day of Atonement. The Jews took seriously the presence of God and His holiness. One of the reasons Jesus was eventually charged by the Jewish religious authorities was His purging of the temple and His claim that it would be destroyed. Read Mark 14:58; 15:29–30; John 2:18–22. What does Jesus teach us about the temple in these passages? Where does the presence of God dwell under the New Testament?

4 Closing

Family Connections

Go over your child's Growing in Christ leaflet together, each of you sharing what you learned about today's Bible story.

This week we see Jesus obeying His parents. He followed the Fourth Commandment perfectly and His perfect obedience is credited to us in Baptism. Though we fail to keep the Fourth Commandment perfectly, Jesus forgives us for those sins of disobedience. Yet He also gives us the Holy Spirit through Word and Sacrament to give us the strength to start obeying His commandments with joyful hearts. We can begin to see parents and others in authority over us as good gifts from God rather than as burdens.

This week, work with your family on memorizing the Fourth Commandment and its explanation from the Small Catechism. Also study Ephesians 6:1–4 together, which teaches about the responsibilities of children to parents and of parents to children. You also may want to look at Luther's Large Catechism on the Fourth Commandment. The Large Catechism is a treasure chest full of insight into the Christian life, just waiting to be tapped into.

Personal Reflection

We have drawn to the close of another calendar year. Many people have made New Year's resolutions. One thing we all know from experience is that we often fail to achieve the goals we set. Falling short and backsliding are particularly frustrating for Christians. Since we have Jesus, shouldn't we make tangible progress at overcoming our failings? Yes and no. The Lord does give us strength through Word and Sacrament to struggle against our old sinful nature, and our lives should show positive results from the Spirit's work in us. But as Paul describes in Romans 7, sinners so often fail to do the good things they want to do and continue to do the things that they know they should not. How frustrating it is to be simultaneously sinner and saint! This constant struggle shows us our need to daily return to Baptism. As Luther says in the Small Catechism, Baptism "indicates that the Old Adam in us should by daily contrition and repentance be drowned and die with all sins and evil desires, and that a new man should daily emerge and arise to live before God in righteousness and purity forever." As you make your plans for the next year, try to include a daily remembrance of your Baptism—one that assures you that you belong to the Lord and also indicates the shape of your Christian life.

For Next Week

The Christmas season draws to a close this coming week as we celebrate the Epiphany of our Lord. Now that we have studied Jesus' birth and childhood, we transition to the season in which Jesus manifests (reveals) who He is. Next week we will study the Baptism of Jesus, in which the Father proclaims to Him, "You are My beloved Son; with You I am well pleased" (Luke 3:22). In preparation for the next lesson, read Luke 3:15–22. If you have time, study the wonders of your own Baptism in Titus 3:5–8.

The Baptism of Jesus

Luke 3:15–22

Key Point

God sent the Holy Spirit at Jesus' Baptism and announced that Jesus was His Son. At my Baptism, God made me His child through the work of the Holy Spirit.

Law/Gospel Point

Because of God's wrath and anger over sin, the people were looking for a Savior. I, too, need a Savior, for God is angry with my sin. **God, in His mercy, makes clear at Jesus' Baptism that they need look no more, for the Savior is here.**

God will divide the wheat from the chaff, the faithful from the unfaithful, gathering the wheat into the barn. **In Baptism, God grants me faith and declares me His child, gathering me into His house.**

Connections

Bible Words

For in Christ Jesus you are all sons of God, through faith. For as many of you as were baptized into Christ have put on Christ. Galatians 3:26–27

Faith Words

sacrament, repent, Epiphany, font

Hymn

Songs of Thankfulness and Praise (*LSB* 394; *LW* 88; *TLH* 134)
To Jordan's River Came Our Lord (*LSB* 405; *HS98* 816)

Catechism

Holy Baptism

Liturgy Link

Sign of the Cross

1 Opening

Today is the first Sunday in the season of Epiphany. Without much thought, Epiphany could be defined as the season that comes between Christmas and Lent. These two times of the Church Year have themes that are so clearly defined, and so easily distinguished that we remember them without difficulty. For some reason, the particular themes of Epiphany, however, escape us. Perhaps Epiphany might be more thoroughly understood if we had a better understanding of the word itself.

Epiphany is a perfectly good word even outside of its connection to the Church Year. If you have a revelation, a moment when something all suddenly becomes crystal clear—an ah-ha moment—then you have had an epiphany. When you see more than you ever expected to see and comprehend the world and your existence in a new way, then you have experienced an epiphany.

With this in mind, over the coming weeks of Epiphany, listen carefully for the themes echoed in the appointed readings. Traditional Epiphany themes deal with such things as Jesus being baptized in the Jordan River, His first sign at the wedding in Cana, miraculous healings, and Jesus shining like the sun on the Mount of Transfiguration.

What do they have in common? Each of them gives us a brief revelation of just who this Jesus really is. Born in a cowshed; raised by ordinary, blue-collar parents; learning and using the skills of a carpenter—it would be easy to forget that Jesus' glory as true God is being intentionally, if temporarily, hidden.

All the participants in the narratives we read during Epiphany saw only momentary glimpses of Jesus' glory. Through God's Word, we live in the light of a much greater revelation of who Jesus is. We see the fullness of His glory as we learn of His life, death, resurrection, and continued saving presence in the Church. Today, we celebrate an epiphany of Jesus as He is baptized in the Jordan River by John the Baptist.

1. Why is the Baptism of Jesus such an appropriate lesson for the Epiphany season?

2. God's Word does not prescribe a certain style or location for a baptismal font in a church. Yet some congregations have large, beautifully designed fonts, and some put the font in a prominent location, such as right inside the entrance to the sanctuary. Why would they do these things? How could the style or location of the font communicate what a congregation believes about Baptism?

2 God Speaks

The Baptism of Jesus
Luke 3:15–22

Law
John's message applies to us, for we are sinners who need to repent.

Gospel
In Baptism, God grants me faith and declares me His child, gathering me into His house.

Context
Epiphany shines forth with the divine glory of the Christ. Here, God the Father acknowledges that Jesus is His Son. John the Baptist has been preaching repentance and baptizing in the Jordan. Now sinless Jesus presents Himself for Baptism. In Baptism, our sins become His, and His righteousness becomes ours.

Commentary
All the people were in great anticipation. There had been no prophet in Israel for four hundred years. Might John be the promised Messiah? John said no. The Messiah would be greater than he, baptizing with the Holy Spirit and fire.

John called people to repentance, for all have sinned and fall short of the glory of God. Like all the prophets, he also proclaimed the forgiveness of sins. So this text is accurate in saying that John "preached good news to the people" (Luke 3:18). John also described the coming Messiah as a righteous judge who would separate the wheat from the chaff—the good from the evil—at the end of the world (Luke 3:17).

The Messiah would baptize "with the Holy Spirit and with fire" (Luke 3:16). First, Jesus would undergo this Baptism Himself. Here, He is baptized with the Holy Spirit in the Jordan. At the cross, He would undergo the destroying fire of God's wrath for sin. All the benefits of Christ's death and resurrection are sealed to you in Baptism. You receive the gift of the Holy Spirit. In Baptism, Christ takes you through the fire with Him as you are killed, buried, and raised again to new life.

Here are some helpful distinctions:

John's Baptism was with water; Jesus' Baptism was with the Holy Spirit and fire.

John's Baptism was preparatory; Jesus' Baptism was the fulfillment of a promise.

John's Baptism was administered by John; Jesus' Baptism is administered by His followers with full authority from the Master: "Whoever receives you receives Me, and whoever receives Me receives Him who sent Me" (Matthew 10:40).

All four Gospels describe the Baptism of Jesus. Luke is unique in putting it in the past tense. Why? His focus is not on the person of John or on the act of Baptism per se. His focus is on the other two persons of the Holy Trinity, who attest to the messianic identity of Jesus. First, we see the Holy Spirit descend on Jesus "in bodily form, like a dove" (Luke 3:22). Why a dove? Of all animals, it represents peace. It was a dove with an olive branch that told Noah that God's wrath in the flood was ended. Thus the Holy Spirit comes upon Jesus and remains. The word *Messiah* means "anointed." Old Testament kings were anointed with oil. But the Messiah is anointed with the Holy Spirit, as this passage shows. Then comes the voice of God the Father from heaven, saying, "You are My beloved Son; with You I am well pleased" (Luke 3:22). God acknowledges the divine and human nature of His only-begotten Son with words very similar to those He would utter at the transfiguration (9:35). Who can doubt the doctrine of the Trinity when we have such a clear passage in which all three persons are present yet functioning in distinct ways? To all who are baptized into Christ, God says, "You are My beloved child."

Discussion questions

1. How does John make it clear that he is not the Christ (Messiah)? See Luke 3:15–16 and John 3:28–30. In what way are pastors like John the Baptist?

2. What did John's Baptism do for those who received it? See Luke 3:3. Jesus was born sinless and never sinned. Why would He, the sinless One, need such a Baptism? See Matthew 3:14–15. What does His Baptism mean for us? See 2 Corinthians 5:17–21.

3. What do we learn from the Old Testament passage that provides the background for Luke 3:22? See Isaiah 42:1. What is the significance for us of the Spirit's descent upon Jesus in the form of a dove? See Luke 3:16 and John 3:5. Based on the Holy Spirit's name, how do we know what He does?

4. How does Christ's Baptism provide insight into to the mission of the apostles and their successors in the Church? See Matthew 28:19–20 and Acts 2:38.

3 We Live

1. Read Luke 3:17. What does this passage say is part of Jesus' mission? Why is this message unpopular today? Why is it important that we continue to proclaim this aspect of Jesus' work?

2. In the early days of Christianity, some churches would not allow people to pray the Lord's Prayer until they were baptized. This might sound strange to us, but if we read the Lord's Prayer closely, we might understand their practice better. Compare the following parts of the Lord's Prayer with the corresponding verses and try to find the connection between them.

"Our Father who art in heaven." See Galatians 3:26–27 and Luke 3:22.

"Hallowed be Thy name." See Matthew 28:19–20 and John 1:12–13.

"Thy kingdom come." See John 3:5.

"Forgive us our trespasses." See Acts 2:38.

4 Closing

Family Connections

Go over your child's Growing in Christ leaflet together, each of you sharing what you learned about today's Bible story.

This week, our lesson discussed how Jesus underwent a Baptism intended for sinners in order to exchange His righteousness for our sin. Martin Luther gives a wonderful exposition of what our Baptism means in the Small Catechism. Review this section of the Small Catechism in your family devotions this week and work on memorizing these great words.

Personal Reflection

Let's face it: we don't think of our Baptism very often. It seems like an event way in the past that has no ongoing significance. Yet Luther explains in the Small Catechism that Baptism "works forgiveness of sins, rescues from death and the devil, and gives eternal salvation to all who believe this, as the words and promises of God declare." Wow! It does all that? Pretty amazing stuff! We'd do well to think of Baptism often.

In the Daily Prayers section of the Small Catechism, Luther suggests that Christians begin their day with prayer and the remembrance of Baptism. "In the morning when you get up, make the sign of the holy cross and say: In the name of the Father and of the Son and of the Holy Spirit. Amen." In the cleansing flood of Baptism, we are united with Christ's death and resurrection. We receive the benefits of His work on the cross, the forgiveness of sins.

In his flood prayer, which is part of the Baptismal rite in *Lutheran Service Book*, Luther says, "Through the Baptism in the Jordan of Your beloved Son, our Lord Jesus Christ, You sanctified and instituted all waters to be a blessed flood and a lavish washing away of sin" (p. 269). With this in mind, what could be another way to remember your Baptism on a daily basis?

Luther says in the Large Catechism: "When our sins and conscience oppress us, we strengthen ourselves and take comfort and say, 'Nevertheless, I am baptized. And if I am baptized, it is promised to me that I shall be saved and have eternal life, both in soul and body.'" Baptism is always in the present tense. "I *am* baptized!" It is a rock-solid, unshakeable foundation for us even when everything else in our lives seems unstable. Such a great thing is this Baptism!

For Next Week

This week, we saw Jesus revealed as the Son of God in His Baptism. Next week, we will see Him performing a miraculous sign that reveals His divine glory. At the wedding at Cana, we see water turned into wine in anticipation of the wine of the New Testament. We also foresee the marriage of Christ to the Church and the eternal wedding banquet of the Lamb. Read John 2:1–11 in preparation for next week's lesson.

Jesus Changes Water into Wine

John 2:1–11

Key Point

Through His first miracle, Jesus revealed Himself to be true God. God uses His Word and physical means—water, bread, and wine—to reveal to me that Jesus is my Savior.

Law/Gospel Points

Like the disciples, I am unsure who Jesus is. **In His Word and Sacraments, Jesus shows me that He is the Savior, as He showed the disciples through His Word and miracles.**

Because of my sin, Jesus had to be true man in order to suffer and die for me. **Jesus was true God who had the power to defeat sin and death.**

In sin, I doubt Jesus and His Word of grace. **God conquers my doubt by showing Himself and His gifts in visible means. I hear Him in His Word and see Him in His Sacraments.**

Connections

Bible Words

And we know that the Son of God has come and has given us understanding, . . . His Son Jesus Christ. . . . is the true God and eternal life. 1 John 5:20

Faith Words

miracle, manifest, glory, attribute

Hymn

Songs of Thankfulness and Praise (*LSB* 394; *LW* 88; *TLH* 134)

Catechism

Apostles' Creed: Second Article

1 Opening

1. In Jesus' day, weddings were occasions for great feasts, often lasting several days. Sometimes we forget the true humanity of Jesus, but we see it in His attendance at the wedding at Cana. No doubt He took part in the festivities, enjoying the delicious food and wine and having a wonderful time with His friends. At another time, we see Jesus go off into the wilderness to fast for forty days. And later, we see His great agony in the garden of Gethsemane and in His Passion. How are these different parts of Jesus' life typical of our own lives?

2. Jesus performed an amazing miracle at the wedding at Cana by changing water into wine. This demonstrated His divine attribute of omnipotence, that is, being all-powerful. How does Jesus use His omnipotence today for our benefit?

3. In John 2:10, the master of the feast tells the bridegroom, "Everyone serves the good wine first, and when people have drunk freely, then the poor wine." Concerning our human nature, of what does this remind us?

2 God Speaks

Jesus Changes Water into Wine
John 2:1–11

Law

We, like the steward of the wedding feast, are often lacking in our preparation for the coming of the Lord.

Gospel

Jesus reveals His divine nature by performing a miracle.

Context

This event occurs at the beginning of Jesus' Galilean ministry. The Scripture lessons of Epiphany demonstrate the glory and divinity of Christ. This one shows His glory through His first miracle.

Commentary

An ancient Jewish wedding custom, betrothal *was* the marriage contract and could not be broken except by divorce. After a period of time, the groom and his friends would go to the home of the bride and bring her and her friends to his home. There they would have a feast, and the couple would begin living together without further ceremony. The feast would often last for days or even a week.

Christ, our Bridegroom, is betrothed to His bride, the Church. Nothing can break His holy vow to take us as His own. Now we are in the waiting time as the Bridegroom prepares a home for us to live in forever (John 14:1–4).

Meanwhile, we are inviting guests by the work of evangelism. At the Last Day, Jesus will appear with all the company of heaven and take us to Himself, and the wedding feast will commence. We will have table fellowship with our Lord in the everlasting banquet (Revelation 19:6–10).

In this text, we see that Mary was there. She was possibly a friend of the bridal couple, since she seems to have had some involvement in the banquet and so was aware of the problem with the wine running low. Jesus is an invited guest along with His six disciples. This event takes place early in His ministry, and the full complement of twelve had not yet been chosen.

The lack of wine was a serious problem and shows a lack of preparation on the part of the steward of the wedding feast or of the groom. It would have caused acute embarrassment. This theme of unpreparedness is similar to the parable of the ten virgins in Matthew 25. Note also the anxiety connected with wedding feasts in other parables of Jesus, such as Matthew 22 and Luke 14. Similarly, we sin by our lack of faith and readiness to receive our Lord. We, too, need to repent, for if Christ were to return this instant, none of us would be ready. Only by grace are we made acceptable in His sight.

Jesus politely yet directly addresses His mother that this current crisis that concerned her did not mean that the hour of His glory had fully arrived. "My hour has not yet come" points her and us to the time of His cross and resurrection. Mary's action, however, in going to Jesus, models prayer. In effect, it is the prayer of "Thy will be done." She evidences this trust (or faith) in Jesus when she tells the servants, "Do whatever He tells you" (John 2:5).

There were six large stoneware jars for water, which the Jews used in their many ceremonial washings. Jesus commanded the servants to fill them, and Jesus turned that water into about 110 gallons (estimates vary) of premium wine, astonishing the steward, the groom, and all present.

The text concludes by saying that there were two results of this miracle. One is that it revealed the glory of the Lord and demonstrated the divinity of Jesus. That is the function of all miracles—to confirm the truth of the words of the prophet. The second result is that the disciples believed in Jesus. So, too, when we learn of the signs that Jesus did, we find that God strengthens our faith by the power of His Word.

Discussion questions

In order to interpret John's Gospel, it is important to understand how he arranges his material. The structure of John's Gospel can be outlined in this way:

I. Prologue (1:1–18)
II. Book of Signs (1:19–12:50)
    a. Miracle at Cana (2:1–11)
    b. Healing of the official's son (4:46–54)
    c. Healing at Bethesda (5:1–17)
    d. Feeding of the five thousand (6:1–15)
    e. Walking on water (6:16–21)
    f. Healing of the blind man (9:1–41)
    g. The raising of Lazarus (11:38–44)
III. Book of Glory (12–20)
    a. Hour of glorification (12)
    b. The farewell discourse / high priestly prayer (17)
    c. Passion (18–19)
    d. Resurrection (20)
IV. Epilogue (21)

It is commonly said that the wedding at Cana was recorded to demonstrate Jesus' divinity. This is true but does not tell the whole story. As we see in the outline above, the Book of Signs is made up of seven signs. (The number 7 often indicates completeness in the Bible.) The miracle at Cana is said in John 2:11 to be the "first of His signs." That also could be translated as the "chief of His signs" or "source of His signs."

1. Based on this observation, what can we say about the significance of the sign He performed at Cana? How did this sign function for His disciples? See John 1:50 and 2:11. How does it function for us? See John 20:30–31.

2. We have seen above that the purpose of the miracle at Cana—and all the other signs—is to reveal Jesus' glory and strengthen the faith of His followers. Read Isaiah 25:6 and Amos 9:13, two prophecies related to the expected age of the Messiah. What about Jesus' miracle at Cana, in particular, revealed His glory and showed that the Messiah had come? Compare Mark 2:22 with this miracle. What do the old wineskins and Jewish purification jars represent? What do the "new wine and wineskins" and "the good wine kept until now" represent?

3. Read Isaiah 62:5 and Jeremiah 2:2. How do these Old Testament passages describe the relationship between God and His people? Why is a wedding such an appropriate place for Jesus to manifest—to reveal—His glory? How is Jesus described in John 3:29? Who is the bride? See Ephesians 5:25–27.

4. When a concept is introduced early on in John's Gospel and recurs repeatedly throughout, this often leads to a very important point later. Two of these words are *hour* and *glory*, both words that appear in John 2:1–11. Read the following passages that mention the hour of Jesus: John 7:30; 12:23–24; 13:1; 17:1. What is Jesus' hour in these verses? How does this shed light on what Jesus means by His hour in John 2:4?

5. We noted above that the first part of John's Gospel is called the Book of Signs and the second is the Book of Glory. Read John 1:14; 2:11; and 8:54 for references to Jesus' glory in the first part of John. Then reread John 12:23–24 and 17:1. Why is it significant that the words *glory* and *hour* appear together in these verses? Read John 19:2–3, 19. In what way is Jesus portrayed as a king? Why is it so shocking that Jesus' glory is to be found at the hour of His crucifixion?

3 We Live

1. We saw above that Jesus' signs reveal who He is for the disciples and for us. Yet not everyone got His signs. Often people missed the underlying meaning. Read John 6:26, 34–35. Why were the people seeking Jesus? What was the true meaning of the sign that He had performed (the feeding of the five thousand)? How does focusing solely on the miraculous nature of Jesus' signs continue to lead people astray today?

2. The purification jars mentioned in John 2:6 represent the ceremonies of the Old Testament, while the wine Jesus creates from the water in them is a sign that the New Testament has come. What did the Jews do with those purification jars? What is this suggestive of under the New Testament? According to Ephesians 5:25–27, what does Christ, the Bridegroom, do for His Bride, the Church?

3. Wine, light, water, and food are symbols of salvation in John's writings. When God's Word is attached to water, it becomes Baptism, a vehicle of salvation—a means of grace. When the Word is attached to bread and wine, it becomes the Lord's Supper, another vehicle of salvation—a means of grace. Read John 19:34–35; 1 John 1:7; 5:6–8. What do these passages teach us about the Lord's appointed means of grace?

4 Closing

Family Connections

Go over your child's Growing in Christ leaflet together, each of you sharing what you learned about today's Bible story.

The wedding at Cana provides a wonderful picture of both the true humanity of Jesus and His true divinity. The Second Article of the Apostles' Creed also clearly confesses Jesus' two natures. This week, recite the Apostles' Creed during your family devotions and also say Luther's Explanation of the Second Article together.

Personal Reflection

The Rite of Holy Matrimony in the Lutheran Service Book Agenda begins:

> Dearly beloved, we are gathered here in the sight of God and before His Church to witness the union of this man and this woman in Holy Matrimony. This is an honorable estate instituted and blessed by God in paradise, before humanity's fall into sin.
>
> In marriage we see a picture of the communion between Christ and His Bride, the Church. Our Lord blessed and honored marriage with His presence and first miracle at Cana in Galilee.

It is worth reminding ourselves often that our Lord has given such a ringing endorsement to marriage. Every Christian marriage should be a sign to the world of the love of Christ for His Church.

This week, consider including in your daily prayers a petition that God would uphold the marriages of your friends and family. If you are married, say a prayer of thanksgiving for God's wonderful gift of marriage.

For Next Week

Today, we saw Jesus reveal His glory, and the disciples believed in Him. Next week, we will see people in His own city of Nazareth reject Him, even though He reveals who He is through the prophet Isaiah's words. In Nazareth, throughout His ministry, and even today, Jesus is rejected by people who do not have faith in Him. Read Luke 4:16–30 in preparation for next week's lesson.

Jesus Rejected at Nazareth

Luke 4:16–30

Key Point

In Nazareth, throughout His ministry, and even today, Jesus is rejected by people who do not have faith in Him. God's Word clearly shows that Jesus is God's Son, and in faith, we believe.

Law/Gospel Points

Sin blinds my eyes to the Savior. **Through God's Word and Sacraments, I can see and believe in Jesus.**

Because of my sinful weakness, I want God to show me His power with a miracle. **God, through water and His Word, has performed the greatest miracle for me, granting me forgiveness and eternal life with Him.**

Connections

Bible Words

All we like sheep have gone astray; we have turned everyone to his own way; and the LORD has laid on Him the iniquity of us all. Isaiah 53:6

Faith Words

synagogue, Gentiles, iniquity, rejected

Hymn

O Morning Star, How Fair and Bright (*LSB* 395; *LW* 73)

Catechism

Lord's Prayer: Third Petition

Liturgy Link

The Sermon

1 Opening

We see in today's lesson that Jesus went to the synagogue on the Sabbath in order to preach. The word *synagogue* comes from Greek, meaning a "gathering of things" or an "assembly of people." The Jewish synagogue was both the local congregation of Jews who prayed, read Scripture, and heard teaching, as well as the place where the congregation assembled. The Sabbath was the weekly day of rest and abstention from work required of the Israelites.

1. In the synagogue, Jesus would read Scripture from a scroll and then preach on the text He read. In Romans 10:17, Paul says that "faith comes from hearing, and hearing through the Word of Christ." What was the primary means of teaching in Jesus' time? Were Bibles available to the people? Would many people have been able to read Hebrew? What does this tell us about the importance of preaching in Jesus' ministry and in the New Testament?

2. In Luke 4:24, Jesus literally says, "Amen, I say to you, no prophet is acceptable in his hometown." What does the word *amen* mean? Why is it attached to prayers?

3. Describe the experience of spending time with people who remember what you were like when you were growing up. How does familiarity with a person's background color your image of him or her? What would the people of Nazareth recall about Jesus' childhood? How could this give insight into Jesus' statement, "No prophet is acceptable in his hometown'" (Luke 4:24)?

2 God Speaks

Jesus Rejected at Nazareth
Luke 4:16–30

Law
We, like the people of Nazareth, reject Christ when He calls us to repentance.

Gospel
Christ shows His divinity in words of power and fulfillment of Scripture, and He also shows Himself a rejected prophet who will die for the sins of His people.

Context
In this lesson, we see Jesus' divinity, but we also have a foreshadowing of the rejection and suffering of Jesus, which we will recall in the upcoming season of Lent. Luke sets forth the preparation for Jesus' ministry with his account of the Baptism and temptation (Luke 3:1–4:13). This passage begins Jesus' Galilean ministry, the first major section in Luke (Luke 4:14–9:50), showing the Savior's divine power in word and deed.

Commentary
Jesus has begun His ministry, becoming famous throughout Galilee for His teaching and miracles (Luke 4:14–15). Now He returns to His hometown of Nazareth on the Sabbath. When the time comes for the reading of Scripture, Jesus stands. A visiting rabbi would have been expected to give an extemporaneous interpretation of the lesson. Jesus is given the scroll of Isaiah and reads from chapter 61. This passage is loaded with the vocabulary of the Gospel. Jesus is anointed, that is, He is the promised Messiah. He has a preaching ministry, proclaiming Good News to the poor and liberty to the captives. The Greek word translated "set at liberty" (Luke 4:18) is ordinarily used to describe the release or remission or forgiveness of sins.

Jesus then sits down; it was customary for teachers to sit on a raised platform with the listeners sitting on the floor at their feet. All eyes are fixed on Him in anticipation, for His fame has preceded Him. Jesus then makes the most startling pronouncement, "Today this Scripture has been fulfilled in your hearing" (Luke 4:21). Obviously, this is a synopsis of His entire sermon. Jesus must have fully expounded the text He had just read, explaining how He Himself was the promised deliverer of Israel and Savior of the world. The people react with amazement at His "gracious words" (Luke 4:22), that is, words that convey God's grace and forgiveness.

But every sermon must contain both Law and Gospel. Jesus does not hesitate to call His listeners to repentance. He knows that underneath they are

61

skeptical and hard-hearted. "Jews demand signs" (1 Corinthians 1:22). Not content with the word of grace, they want Jesus to perform a miracle. The formula "Truly, I say to you" (Luke 4:24) always introduces an important saying of Jesus. In Luke, it occurs six times and always at a critical juncture (12:37; 18:17; 18:29; 21:32; 23:43). The last is Jesus' word to the thief on the cross.

In His second discourse, Jesus draws on history to rebuke the unbelief of the Jews and tell them that God is going to open His covenant to the Gentiles. He uses the illustration of Elijah, who was sent to the Gentile widow in Sidon, and goes on to describe how Elisha cleansed Naaman the Syrian from leprosy. Instead of humbly repenting, the people become angry. Note the use of the word *all* in both verses 22 and 28. They throw Jesus out of the city and take Him to a cliff to throw Him down. But the Messiah is in control. He lays down His life; no man takes it from Him until the appointed hour (John 10:18). Ironically, a miracle is performed as Jesus passes through the crowd unharmed and goes on His way.

Discussion questions

Just as the miracle at Cana was the first sign given by Jesus in John's Gospel and set the stage for the other signs, Jesus' proclamation in Luke 4:18–21 defines the pattern of His future ministry. The sermon reveals what Jesus would go on to do and preach. The people's response to His message in Luke 4:28–29 provides a pattern for His future rejection. In this lesson, Jesus identifies Himself as a prophet by describing this pattern of what He will do and experience. The Old Testament prophets taught, worked miracles, and faced rejection from the people to whom they were sent.

1a. What phrases in Luke 4:18–19 indicate that Jesus will be a teacher and work miracles? Read Luke 4:31–37. How does this account in Capernaum revisit the two primary themes from His previous sermon?

1b. According to Luke 4:23, Jesus anticipated that the people of Nazareth would expect Him to perform signs and wonders such as He had done in Capernaum. "Physician, heal yourself" might be a reference to the idea that one should not forget to help his own family and friends while he assists complete strangers. Yet as a prophet, Jesus would fare no better than the prophets of Israel, such as Elijah and Elisha who were often rejected by the people. Therefore, God sent Elijah to the Gentile (non-Israelite) widow in

Zarapheth, and Elisha was given the task of cleansing the pagan Namaan. How does the account in Luke 4:28–29 suggest what will eventually happen to the prophet Jesus? Read Luke 13:31–34.

2. In Luke 4:18, Jesus says that He will "set at liberty those who are oppressed." As has been noted, the Greek word translated as "set at liberty" is often used to describe the forgiveness of sins, so this passage announces one of the major themes of Jesus' preaching. Read Isaiah 53:6, our Bible verse for today. In what way does sin still oppress us? In what sense are we liberated from the oppression of sin? See Luke 1:77 and 24:47.

3. Jesus quotes the Messianic prophecy of Isaiah 61 in Luke 4:18, "The Spirit of the Lord is upon me, because He has anointed Me to proclaim good news to the poor." Who else besides Jesus is mentioned in that verse? What event was a key revelation that Jesus is the promised Anointed One or Messiah? See Luke 3:21–22 and Acts 10:38.

4. The language of Luke 4:18–19 indicates that God has come to restore the fallen creation, to release it from bondage to decay and death. Read Colossians 1:15–20. Who does Paul describe as the Creator of all things? How does the Creator reconcile Himself to the Creator? How does Luke 4:18–19 support the theme of the restored creation?

5. Luke 4:19 says that Jesus came to "proclaim the year of the Lord's favor." The background for this statement is found in Leviticus 25, in which the Jubilee Year is prescribed to the Israelites. Read Leviticus 25:8–10. How often was the Jubilee Year? What occurred during this year? What themes are found in both Leviticus 25:8–10 and Luke 4:18–19?

3 We Live

1. What did Jesus mean in Luke 4:21 that "Today this Scripture has been fulfilled in your hearing"? To which passage does this refer? What does this say about the power of His preaching? What does preaching accomplish in the Church today? See 1 Corinthians 1:21–25.

2. In Luke 4:15–16, we learn that Jesus customarily taught in the Jewish synagogue. He would read the Old Testament and interpret it, revealing Himself as the Messiah. How did Paul and the apostles use the synagogue to expand the Church? See Acts 9:20; 13:5; 14:1 as examples. How does the preaching that Paul did in the synagogues compare with the preaching we hear at church today?

3. In light of Jesus' preaching in Luke 4:18–19, why do we still see the consequences of sin in creation? What does God really desire from us? Read Hebrews 11:1.

4 Closing

Family Connections

Go over your child's Growing in Christ leaflet together, each of you sharing what you learned about today's Bible story.

The misunderstanding of the role of miracles and healing in Jesus' ministry has often led Christians to have false expectations about miracles and healing in their own lives. Though God can and does perform miracles, they are always done by grace. We cannot merit them. We should pray for help and healing but also must always pray, "Thy will be done," recognizing that our Lord knows what we need better than we do ourselves. Luther reminds us in the Small Catechism that God's will is chiefly directed at "keeping us strong in His Word and faith till we die."

Study the Third Petition of the Lord's Prayer from the Small Catechism during your family devotions. Devotions provide important truths about how God's Kingdom has come and continues to come to your family.

Personal Reflection

We saw Jesus today in the synagogue on the Sabbath, attending to God's Word. The Third Commandment is "Remember the Sabbath day by keeping it holy." Luther explains some aspects of this commandment in his Large Catechism:

> Now, in the Old Testament, God set apart the seventh day and appointed it for rest (Genesis 2:3). He commanded that it should be regarded as holy above all other days. This commandment was given only to the Jewish people for this outward obedience, that they should stop toilsome work and rest. . . . This commandment, therefore, in its literal sense, does not apply to us Christians. It is entirely an outward matter, like other ordinances of the Old Testament. The ordinances were attached to particular customs, persons, times, and places, but now they have been made matters of freedom through Christ (LC I 80, 82).

As Paul says, "let no one pass judgment on you in questions of food and drink, or with regard to a festival or a new moon or a Sabbath" (Colossians 2:16). In the Small Catechism, Luther explains how this commandment still applies to us today: "We should fear and love God so that we do not despise preaching and His Word, but hold it sacred and gladly hear and learn it."

For Next Week

Through many miracles, Jesus shows us His power over sin and the devil. Read Luke 4:31–44 in preparation for next week's class.

Jesus Heals Many

Luke 4:31–44

Key Point

Through many miracles, Jesus shows us His power over sin and the devil.

Law/Gospel Point

Because of sin, Satan has power and holds the world in bondage. **Jesus is the Holy One of God who defeats Satan and frees me from his hold, granting me eternal life in paradise.**

Because of sin there is sickness in the world. **Jesus has power over sin and sickness.**

I am lost in sin and death. **Jesus was sent to preach and, through His own suffering and death, to save the lost.**

God wants me and all others to know and believe in His Son. **He speaks through His Word, and, in faith, grants me the opportunities to tell others this Good News about Jesus.**

Connections

Bible Words
When [Jesus] saw their faith, He said, "Man, your sins are forgiven you." Luke 5:20

Faith Words
demon possession, kingdom of God, Satan, condemned

Hymn
O Son of God, in Galilee (*LSB* 841; *LW* 400)

Catechism
Apostles' Creed: Second Article
Lord's Prayer: Seventh Petition

1 Opening

Today's lesson from Luke 4:31–44 has several features that strike our modern sensibilities as just plain odd. Jesus is casting out demons right and left, and they are screaming out that He is the Holy One of God and the Son of God. What are we to make of all of this?

Many modern people live as if nothing exists apart from what they can see. They hold to a philosophy known as materialism. A materialist assumes that if something is not material, it either doesn't exist or we cannot know anything about it. On the other hand, some people are spiritualists and think that matter is either only an illusion or is unimportant. Of course, you can see simply in the person of Jesus Christ evidence against both of these approaches. He is true, material man and also true, spiritual God.

We confess in the Nicene Creed that God created "all things visible and invisible." Angels are completely spiritual beings who are good; demons are totally evil. Angels do God's will; demons do the will of Satan, God's enemy. Previously, we saw the angels bringing messages of joy to Zechariah, Mary, and the shepherds. Today, we see demons bringing nothing but pain and misery to people.

Though we cannot see them, angels and demons still are at work today, doing either God's or Satan's work. Matthew 4:11 says that after the devil stopped tempting Jesus, angels came and served Him. Certainly they do the same for us. Matthew 18:10 says that little children have their very own angels in heaven.

On the other hand, St. Peter tells us to be watchful because our "adversary the devil prowls around like a roaring lion, seeking someone to devour" (1 Peter 5:8). St. Paul tells us to put on the armor of God so that we "may be able to stand against the schemes of the devil. For we do not wrestle against flesh and blood, but against the rulers, against the authorities, against the cosmic powers over this present darkness, against the spiritual forces of evil in the heavenly places" (Ephesians 6:11–12). So much for materialism!

Many Christians spend a lot of time speculating about these spiritual beings, but what is more important to remember is that Christ has conquered the devil and his demons and that God has promised to send angels to watch over us. We pray in Luther's Morning and Evening Prayers, "Let Your holy angel be with me, that the evil foe may have no power over me." God answers that prayer, even when we don't realize it! And He has promised that His Word and Sacraments will be a tangible shield for us against the attacks of Satan. Though the demons still have great power in this world, Jesus is infinitely greater and will not let us be harmed by them. In today's lesson, we see how Jesus demonstrated His authority over the demons, which anticipated His ultimate overcoming of Satan and his servants on the cross.

2 God Speaks

Jesus Heals Many

Luke 4:31–44

Law

Because of sin, Satan has power and holds the world in bondage. Because of sin, there is sickness in the world.

Gospel

Jesus is the Holy One of God, who defeats Satan and frees me from his hold, granting me eternal life in paradise. Jesus has power over sin and sickness. God speaks through His Word and, in faith, grants me opportunities to tell others this Good News about Jesus.

Context

The Epiphany emphasis continues as Christ's preaching and miracles reveal His divinity. These events occur during the time of Jesus' earthly ministry when many were attracted to the miracle-working preacher.

Commentary

The Greek word *epitimao* ("rebuke") is used three times here. Jesus rebukes a demon (Luke 4:35), a fever (Luke 4:39), and many demons (Luke 4:41). He is demonstrating His divine power over the evil effects of sin, whether they be spiritual or physical.

The Greek word *dei* ("must," "necessary") is used to great effect in Luke 4:43, where Jesus says that He *must* preach the kingdom of God to other cities. With this word, Luke connotes the will of God for His Son. We saw this word in Luke 2:49, where Jesus says to His parents that He *must* be about the things of His Father. His entire purpose was to be obedient to His Father and to fulfill the things written about Him by the prophets.

Therefore, it was *necessary* for Him to be in the temple, to preach the Word of God, and to go to the cross and rise again (Luke 24:44). All this was for your benefit, that you might have forgiveness of sins and everlasting life.

As He teaches, people are amazed at the authority of His words (Luke 4:36). He is not like other rabbis, quibbling over controversies. His voice is the voice of God Himself.

First, we see the cleansing of the man with the unclean spirit. Note that he is in the synagogue. The devil is at work in the Church as well as outside it.

The demon cries out and confesses Christ—though not with saving faith. It recognizes that Jesus is "the Holy One of God" (Luke 4:34). At this early point in Jesus' ministry, no human knows who He really is. We don't find that understanding until Peter's confession of Christ in Luke 9:20. Jesus commands the evil spirit to be silent, for it is not yet time for Him to fully reveal Himself. Then Jesus expels the demon, showing His divine power over the forces of darkness. Again the people are astonished, because the authority of His teaching is confirmed by the works of power that He does. No ordinary rabbi could do such things, but only a true prophet sent from God.

The second startling event here is the healing of Peter's mother-in-law. Luke says that Jesus stood over her. Mark, in reporting this incident, says that Jesus took her hand, a lovely detail that shows the tender love of our Savior toward the suffering (Mark 1:31). Luke emphasizes the power and divine authority of Jesus. He rebukes the high fever—she really was seriously ill—and it flees. Then she got up and fixed dinner.

What a day this must have been! At the end of the day, the people brought to Jesus the sick and demon-possessed. He healed them. Again the demons confess His divinity, here calling Him the Son of God. Apparently Jesus ministered all night, for He went off into a deserted place as He did so often to pray and meditate. But the people pursued Him, a stark contrast to the time of His Passion, when all men, including His disciples, would desert Him. Yet by faith we confess His name and worship Him, and strengthened by Word and Sacraments, we remain faithful until death.

Discussion questions

1. In Luke 4:34, the unclean demon cried out to Jesus, "I know who You are—the Holy One of God." Why does this demon cry out when he encounters Jesus? According to James 2:19, what does the knowledge of God cause demons to do? What do the demons in Luke 4:34 and 4:41 tell the reader of Luke's Gospel about Jesus?

2. We see in Luke 4:35 and 4:41 that Jesus will not let the demons speak, "because they knew that He was the Christ." Apparently, Jesus did not want to be revealed as the Christ from the lips of demons. What possible reasons would Jesus have not to be revealed to the world at that time as the Christ? Read Luke 9:18–22. To whom is Jesus revealed as the Christ here? What does Jesus tell them not to do?

What event does Jesus predict but appears not yet ready to undergo? Read John 11:47–48 and Matthew 2:1–4. What do these passages reveal as possible reasons for Jesus to keep a low profile?

3. In Luke 4:43, Jesus says that He was sent to "preach the good news [Gospel] of the kingdom of God." The kingdom of God is an important theme in Luke's Gospel. As Jesus preaches and performs miracles, He is showing that the kingdom of God has arrived. God is bringing about a new creation in Christ Jesus, giving new life to sinners. It is a kingdom of grace, a kingdom of the Gospel. In short, the kingdom of God is found wherever Jesus is King. Read Luke 10:8–12. When Jesus sent out His seventy-two messengers, what signs would accompany their message that the kingdom of God had come? What happens when people rejected that message? Read Luke 18:15–17. How must the kingdom of God be received?

4. Jesus revealed the breaking in of the kingdom of God by showing His great authority. In Luke 4:32, the people were astounded that His Word possessed such authority. He spoke as if He were God Himself, because He is! Then in Luke 4:36, the people were amazed at the authority He exercised over demons. Read Luke 5:17–26. What other authority did Jesus have and why was that so offensive to the scribes and Pharisees? According to John 20:19–23, what authority does Jesus give to the apostles, which is also given to those in the Office of the Holy Ministry?

3 We Live

1. According to Luke 4:36–37, Jesus' authoritative preaching and miracles amazed the people, and "reports about Him went out into every place in the surrounding region." But Jesus had not yet revealed Himself as the Christ.

What kind of faith, if any, could have been present among the people who witnessed these miracles? What warning does Jesus give us about faith healers and miracle workers (Mark 13:21–22)? In contrast, according to Luke 5:24, what is one reason that Jesus did miracles? Would modern faith healers and miracle workers have the same agenda as Jesus did? In what way can Jesus' healing ministry be continued in the Church today?

2. In Luke 4:38–39, Jesus healed Simon's (Peter's) mother-in-law of a high fever. After Jesus rebuked the fever and it left her, "immediately she rose and began to serve them." How does Peter's mother-in-law provide a wonderful example for Christian faith and life? How is this same attitude reflected in the Collect of Thanksgiving that is traditionally used after Holy Communion (*LW* p. 174)?

3. What is one reason why so many people reject the Gospel? Why is it that many people do not go to church or go to churches that focus on things other than the Gospel? See 2 Corinthians 4:4 and Luke 8:12. What is the ultimate source of unbelief? Of what must Christians also be constantly aware?

4. According to Luke 4:40, Jesus would lay His hands on people who were sick and heal them. Jesus comes to us with His true body and blood in the Sacrament of the Altar, forgiving our sins and giving us life and salvation. Martin Luther says in the Large Catechism, "We must never think of the Sacrament [of the Altar] as something harmful from which we had better flee, but as a pure, wholesome, comforting remedy that grants salvation and comfort. It will cure you and give you life both in soul and body. For where the soul has recovered, the body also is relieved" (LC V 68).

According to Luther, what besides the soul can be helped by the Sacrament? How should we be careful in our understanding of this teaching? How does this teaching point to the final resurrection of our bodies?

4 Closing

Family Connections

Go over your child's Growing in Christ leaflet together, each of you sharing what you learned about today's Bible story.

Jesus' preaching and healing ministries were signs that the kingdom of God had arrived. Luther eloquently describes how the Holy Spirit brings the kingdom of God to us in his explanation to the Second Petition of the Lord's Prayer in the Small Catechism. He also reminds us of our constant need for defense against the threats of Satan in his explanation of the Seventh Petition. Use these two parts of the Small Catechism in your family devotions this week, and work on memorizing them.

Personal Reflection

In Greek, the Seventh Petition of the Lord's Prayer reads, "Deliver us from the Evil One." Evil is not some disembodied substance—it is personal. Satan and his demons are very real. This week, pray for defense against the evil one, and find defense in God's Word and your Baptism both at church and in personal devotion.

For Next Week

This week, we continued to see the Epiphany theme of Jesus revealing Himself through preaching and miraculous signs. Next week, we will see how He calls followers who will preach and do miracles in His behalf. We will learn that Jesus chose ordinary, sinful men to follow Him and be His disciples. In Baptism, Jesus chooses us to be His children. In the Church, He continues to choose ordinary, sinful men to serve as His messengers in the Office of the Holy Ministry. Read Luke 5:1–11 in preparation for next week's class.

Jesus Calls the First Disciples

Luke 5:1–11

Key Point

Jesus chose ordinary, sinful men to follow Him and be His disciples. In Baptism, Jesus chooses us to be His children.

Law/Gospel Points

In my sin, I want to hide from Jesus. **In Jesus' forgiveness, I find peace and favor with God.**

Because of sin, I doubt that Jesus is who He says He is. **God's Word testifies repeatedly and consistently that Jesus is God's Son.**

Because of my sin, my work is hard and often unfruitful. **Jesus shows His power over sin and makes my work productive, giving forgiveness, new life, and salvation through His Word and Sacraments.**

Connections

Bible Words

And Jesus said to them, "Follow Me, and I will make you become fishers of men." Mark 1:17

Faith Words

disciple, nave, sins of commission, sins of omission

Hymn

Come, Follow Me, the Savior Spake (*TLH* 421)

Catechism

Apostles' Creed: Third Article
Holy Baptism

1 Opening

Are all of your fish stories happy? Many of us have experienced the disappointment of going fishing and coming home empty-handed or of breaking our fishing pole, losing it in the water, or letting the big one getting away!

At the beginning of our lesson today in Luke 5, Simon is rather discouraged. He has labored all night but has caught no fish. And he's not fishing for pleasure—he's fishing for a living! When a commercial fisherman doesn't catch fish, his family doesn't eat, and he doesn't make any money. But after a long night out, it's time to wash, dry, and put away the nets so he can go home and at least catch a bit of sleep.

But within a few minutes, things for Peter will have made a complete turnaround. Jesus will provide Peter with a record catch and commission him to be a fisher of men. Yet the turnaround will not be without its ups and downs. There will be frustration, sin, shame, and the need for forgiveness before everything ends on a high note.

The story of Joseph in Genesis 37–50 is similar. Perhaps no one in the history of God's people experienced the ups and downs that Joseph did. Scorned by his brothers, thrown into a pit to die, sold into slavery, ascending to a position of power in Egypt only to be imprisoned for a crime he didn't commit, finally being released from prison and returning to a position of influence, eventually reconciled with his brothers—what a roller coaster!

What we see in the lives of Peter and Joseph is pretty familiar, isn't it? We go through periods of great disappointment and frustration and also times of joy. The life of the Christian cannot be one unbroken string of successes and happy times, for we are continually being conformed to our Lord Jesus (Romans 8:29). He, too, had great ups and downs in His life, much more extreme than we ever could experience. The greatest down was His shameful death on the cross, bearing the weight of our sins. The greatest up was His glorious resurrection in which He declared us righteous—forgiven of all our sins and heirs of His glory.

No matter how wild the ups and downs of life, we follow in the footsteps of our Lord, who brings us safely along our journey of life just as He did for Peter.

2 God Speaks

Jesus Calls the First Disciples

Luke 5:1–11

Law

We, like Peter, can all say, "I am a sinner."

Gospel

As Jesus says to us, "Fear not," He absolves us of our sins and commissions us to call others to Christ.

Context

This lesson continues the Epiphany glory theme with the miraculous catch. In this lesson, Christ begins establishing the apostolic foundation of the Church by calling Peter, James, and John.

Commentary

The preaching ministry of Jesus continues (Luke 4:31, 43–44). A key word in this passage is *akouo* ("hear"), the Greek equivalent of the Hebrew *shema* ("hear"), which occurs frequently in the Old Testament. God is delivering His Word to His people and making disciples by the formation of their minds and hearts and actions. The people are following a rabbi, Jesus. They hear His Word and apply it in their lives. In the Church, we call this catechesis.

The crowds are pressing in on Jesus to hear His teaching as He stands by Lake Gennesaret (the Sea of Galilee). He gets into Simon's boat and tells him to shove off. Then Jesus sits down and teaches from the boat. Sound carries well over the hard surface of water, so this would have been a practical way for our Lord to address the large crowds. The boat imagery is biblical. Noah and his family and the animals were saved by means of a ship. Likewise, the place in church where everybody sits is called the nave, from the Latin *navis* ("ship"). Christ saves those within the ship.

When I lived in Florida, I used to watch the mullet fishermen. They worked in small boats with nets, fishing close to shore at night. That is when and where the mullet were feeding. Here, in the Bible account, an experienced crew of fishermen has been out working during the most propitious time for fishing and had no success.

Then comes the account of the miraculous catch of fish. The close observer will note that Peter has been in the boat listening to the words of Jesus. He, a man, has already been caught. Jesus tells him to put out into the deep part of the lake and let down his nets. This runs counter to human wisdom, but Peter, after a halfhearted protest, obeys. Suddenly, he finds that his nets are so full they are about to break. He calls his partners, and they fill both boats with fish.

Peter's reaction is instructive. He knows from this miracle that Jesus must be some kind of prophet or holy man—remember that his confession of Jesus as the Christ does not come until Luke 9—and he reacts in fear, confessing himself to be a sinner. His partners also are filled with amazement. Jesus quickly absolves them of their sins with the words "Do not be afraid" (Luke 5:10); just as quickly, He gives them a commission to go and absolve the sins of others: "From now on you will be catching men" (Luke 5:10). The Greek is vivid here. It literally means "catch alive." When you catch a fish, it is alive, and then it dies. When you catch a man for Christ, he is dead in sins but then becomes alive through new birth in Baptism.

Discussion questions

1. Read Matthew 4:18–22. Does Matthew refer to the same event as Luke 5:1–11? What are the key differences between these stories? What is the difference between Jesus saying, "I will make you fishers of men" (Matthew 4:19) and "From now on you will be catching men" (Luke 5:10)?

2. The people had been astonished by the authority with which Jesus proclaimed the Word (Luke 4:32). Note that in Luke 5:1, the people are gathered around Him to "hear the word of God." Luke is making it clear that, from Jesus' time onward, hearing the Word of God is the same as hearing the Word of Jesus. Read Luke 8:21 and 11:28. What does Jesus say about those who receive His Word in faith? How does this message apply to us?

Simon (Peter) is one of the central persons in this lesson. He is mentioned in 5:3, 4, 5, 8, and 10. He was a leader among the Twelve. He often would answer questions from Jesus on behalf of the disciples and made the great confession that Jesus is the Christ, the Son of the living God (Matthew 16:16). Immediately after that confession, Peter denies that Jesus could suffer and die (Matthew 16:22). Before Jesus' death, Peter denies Him three times (Luke 22:56–62). In today's lesson, Peter is specifically called by Jesus. We see traces of his faithfulness and faithlessness throughout. After the frustrating night of not catching anything, it was a burden for Peter to put the nets back out in the deep, for they had already been washed and it was time to go home. Yet he grudgingly obeys Jesus' command. Then the Word of Jesus creates the great catch of fish. Whatever Peter may have expected, amazement seizes him and the others with the great catch Jesus provides. Immediately, Peter becomes ashamed for doubting Jesus. He finds himself a total sinner in the face of the Holy One of God.

3. Read Isaiah 6:1–7. How was Isaiah's experience similar to Peter's? How were Isaiah and Peter both comforted? What do these stories tell us about God?

4. In Luke 5:10, Jesus tells Simon that he will begin catching men. In order to catch fish, you need a net and a boat. To catch men, Peter needed a means of catching people and a way to keep them alive. Read Acts 2:14, 36–42. What net does Peter use to catch people? Where were the people kept alive? How does this fishing expedition continue today?

5. Read Matthew 13:47–50. Though this parable is not a direct parallel to the story in Luke 5, it uses similar fishing imagery. What sobering fact does it teach us about the Church's catch of men?

3 We Live

1. In today's story, the fishermen fished with nets, not lines and hooks. Why is the image of a net bringing us into the Church more comforting than a hook?

2. Jesus brought about the miraculous catch of fish by His almighty power. In fact, the Greek does not say that the fishermen caught the fish but that the nets enclosed them. It was not an active accomplishment on the part of the fishermen. What comforting fact does this tell us about the mission of the Church?

3. Why would it not make much sense if every person was a professional fisherman? Why isn't every Christian specifically called to be a fisher of men in the Office of the Holy Ministry?

4 Closing

Family Connections

Go over your child's Growing in Christ leaflet together, each of you sharing what you learned about today's Bible story.

Today's story describes the commissioning of Peter to catch men by preaching the Gospel and administering the Sacraments. This certainly makes us think of Holy Baptism, which is, as Luther says, "a gracious water of life and a washing of regeneration in the Holy Spirit" (SC IV). The Holy Spirit works through Word and Sacrament to accomplish His work of building the Church. We confess in the Third Article of the Apostles' Creed, "I believe in the Holy Spirit, the holy Christian Church, the communion of saints, the forgiveness of sins, and the life everlasting." The Holy Spirit works in the Church to create a communion of saints by the forgiveness of sins so He can give people life everlasting. Review the Baptism and Third Article of the Creed sections of the Small Catechism in your family devotions this week and work on memorizing them.

Personal Reflection

In today's lesson, Simon (Peter) takes a journey without really going anywhere. He goes from calling Jesus "Master" to calling Him "Lord."

In Luke 5:5, Simon says, "Master, we toiled all night and took nothing! But at Your word I will let down the nets." His words belie a sense of obligation to obey what Jesus says. He doesn't really think they will catch any fish but does it anyway. He views Jesus as His Master and himself as a servant.

After Jesus finished talking to the crowd, He remained seated but began to speak directly to Simon. As the miraculous catch happened, Simon realized his sinfulness. He knew that he had not trusted in the Word of his Master. He recognized that he had acted like an unbelieving slave, not as a believing son. In spite of Simon's faithlessness, Jesus still gave him an overabundance of fish. And then an amazing change came over Simon. The Holy Spirit inspired Luke to call Simon *Peter* in Luke 5:8. Previously, Luke had called him Simon three times in this lesson. Suddenly Luke says, "When Simon *Peter* saw it, he fell down at Jesus' knees, saying 'Depart from me, for I am a sinful man, O Lord'" (Luke 5:8). For the first time in his Gospel, Luke calls Simon "Peter," which is the name that Jesus gave him on the first day He met him (John 1:42). It is also the name Jesus calls Peter after he makes the confession that Jesus is the Christ—the solid rock confession on which Jesus will build His Church (Matthew 16:18)!

How was Simon changed to Peter? The grace of Christ! Jesus dealt with Simon by grace, showing him that he no longer needed to live as a slave but as a son.

Jesus does for us far more than we could ever ask or even think, just like He did for Peter. This week, reflect on all the times the Lord has blessed you in spite of yourself, the times He has not dealt with you on the basis of your sins, and the times you have felt that you don't deserve such a gracious Lord. Jesus is the One who came to bear your sins, to absolve you of them, and to set you free from them. He is not a harsh and cruel Master, but a gracious and loving Lord. Jesus always wants the last Word that you hear from Him to be Gospel, not Law!

For Next Week

As a prophet, Jesus both performed miracles and taught the Word of God. This week, we saw Jesus' gift of a miraculous catch of fish for a downhearted fisherman who would soon become a fisher of men as he was sent out to proclaim God's Word. Next week, we will hear Jesus teaching some of the most profound words ever recorded. We will study the Beatitudes, Matthew 5:1–12, in which Jesus explains that He was poor, hungry, sorrowful, hated, and rejected for our sake so that God would grant us His gifts and blessings. Read this passage in preparation for next week, and if you have time, read the entire Sermon on the Mount, recorded in Matthew 5–7.

The Beatitudes
Matthew 5:1–12

Key Point

Jesus explains in His Word that He was poor, hungry, sorrowful, hated, and rejected for our sake so that God would grant us His gifts and blessings.

Law/Gospel Points

I deserve nothing but sorrow and trouble because of my sin. **Jesus, in His love, took my sorrow, trouble, and sin upon Himself that I might have a heavenly reward.**

In this world, I will suffer and struggle because of my sin. **God's Word assures me that in Jesus, eternal life in heaven will be mine.**

In my sin, I am declared unrighteous before God. **A beatitude is a declaration of blessedness for those who believe in Jesus.**

Connections

Bible Words

Surely He has borne our griefs and carried our sorrows. Isaiah 53:4

Faith Words

beatitudes, blessed, merciful, persecution

Hymn

All Depends on Our Possessing (*LSB* 732; *LW* 415; *TLH* 425)
The Gifts Christ Freely Gives Us (*LSB* 602)

Catechism

Lord's Prayer: Second Petition
Apostles' Creed: Second Article

Liturgy

The Benediction

1 Opening

For centuries, the Beatitudes have been the Gospel reading for All Saints' Day. They have been labeled "the definition of a saint." But when you read the Beatitudes, it is impossible to see how *anyone* could be a saint based on the expectations they set forth. They pronounce as blessed only the poor in spirit, the meek, those who hunger and thirst after righteousness, those who mourn, the merciful, the pure in heart, the peacemakers, and the persecuted. Where does that leave us with our arrogant spirits, obstinate—not meek—wills, hungering and thirsting after evil, rejoicing in our sins but not mourning them, ruthlessness not mercy, lustful rather than pure hearts, making war not peace, and avoiding persecution rather than suffering for Christ's name?

"Lord, have mercy!" is the only thing we can cry. But often we try another line of defense against the radical standards set by the Beatitudes. We try to explain them away by reinterpreting the words to lessen the demands. The problem is, Jesus means what He says. He does expect those things of us. He teaches later in Matthew, "You therefore must be perfect, as your heavenly Father is perfect" (5:48). Ouch! Does it get any more demanding than that? We cannot just try hard enough to fulfill the standards of the Beatitudes and to be perfect. That's clearly not good enough. The bar has been raised, and we cannot reach it.

1. In light of what you have just read, in what way can the Beatitudes properly be called "the definition of a saint"?

2. If you work hard at your job, you often will get promoted. The world usually blesses diligence. How does Jesus' description of blessedness in the Beatitudes differ from the world's views? According to Matthew 16:16–17, what is the only source of blessing?

2 God Speaks

The Beatitudes

Matthew 5:1–12

Law

I deserve nothing but sorrow and trouble because of my sin. Trusting in my own ways, riches, confidence, and influence, I am blinded by sin.

Gospel

Jesus, in His love, took my sorrow, trouble, and sin upon Himself that I might have a heavenly reward. Jesus offers all things through faith in Him, granting me eternal riches and blessings.

Context

The season of Epiphany is drawing to a close, continuing to emphasize the divine power of Jesus. Jesus with His twelve apostles comes down from the mountain and continues His powerful ministry of healing and teaching.

Commentary

Even though Jesus has power to heal, the greatest gift He brings to suffering humanity is His Word. Those He heals of one disease will succumb to another. Those He raises from the dead will one day die again. But those He brings to faith will have comfort in this life and untold blessings in the world to come.

The Greek word *makarios* ("blessed") is a "declaration of blessedness" upon the person who is in communion with God through Jesus Christ. There are many beatitudes in the Bible, and fifteen in Luke's Gospel (1:45; 6:20–22; 7:23; 10:23; 11:27–28; 12:37–38, 43; 14:14–15; 23:29).

In the kingdom of God, the hungry are filled, the mourning rejoice, the last become first, and God chooses the foolish to shame the wise and learned.

The Beatitudes are Christological; all of them apply to Jesus. He was poor and hungry, a man of sorrows acquainted with grief. Yet it was for the joy set before Him that He endured the cross, despising its shame. He now sits at the right hand of God. He was hated, despised, rejected, cast out, beaten, spat upon, and crucified. Yet now, risen from the dead, He has a name that is above all other names. Upon hearing it, every knee shall bow in heaven and on earth, and everyone will confess that Jesus Christ is Lord to the glory of the Father.

The Beatitudes are Gospel. Do not turn them into Law. They are descriptive, not prescriptive. They show what life is like in Christ. Things may be bad for you in this life, but in the life to come you will have joy forevermore.

Finally, the Beatitudes are both spiritual and physical in their meaning. Luke says, "Blessed are the poor"; Matthew says, "Blessed are the poor in spirit." Both are true.

Regarding the hungry, this applies as well to those who are literally hungry and those who are spiritually hungry. Jesus fed the five thousand, and they were filled. The Greek word *chortazo* ("fill") is used in both places. This vivid word derives from *chortos* ("grass") and indicates a state of being full like a cow that has eaten so much it couldn't possibly hold another bite. By grace we hunger after the things of God, and He fills us to the brim.

Likewise with those who weep. Everyone in the world has trouble and sorrow, and God uses those troubles to draw people to Himself through Christ. In the words of an old spiritual, "Nobody knows the troubles I've seen, nobody knows but Jesus." In the arms of our Suffering Servant Savior, we find comfort and consolation. At the same time, our deepest grief is over our sins. Yet Jesus Christ takes our sins upon His own body on the cross and gives us the same beatitude He gave the thief: "Today you will be with Me in paradise."

Discussion questions

We have asserted above that the Beatitudes are Christological, and that all of them apply to Jesus. Yet you will notice that the first eight Beatitudes are written in the third person plural—referring to "they" or "theirs." In spite of being plural, they primarily refer to Christ, since only He lived them out perfectly. In this section, we will look at each Beatitude individually and see how Jesus embodied each of them, fulfilling their demands in our place. Yet since they are written in the plural, the Holy Spirit also uses the Words and deeds of Jesus to teach us what a life of Christian love looks like. Nevertheless, we live in complete reliance on Christ's mercy, for we sin much as we live out our Christian lives.

1. The first Beatitude is "Blessed are the poor in spirit, for theirs is the kingdom of heaven" (Matthew 5:3). Jesus opens His first public sermon with these words, so they must be important. It is easy to understand financial poverty, but much harder to comprehend spiritual poverty. In this case, being poor in spirit refers to how a person stands before God. The poor in spirit do not make any claims on God but stand before Him as beggars who expect no rewards. The kingdom of heaven cannot be a reward for works but is God's work in Jesus to save the world. According to 2 Corinthians 8:9 and Matthew 20:25–28, how does Jesus live out this Beatitude?

2. The second Beatitude is "Blessed are those who mourn, for they shall be comforted" (Matthew 5:4). For whom does Jesus mourn in Matthew 23:37 and Isaiah 53:4? According to Isaiah 61:1–2, why did Jesus receive the Spirit? According to Revelation 21:4, what promise does Jesus make?

3. The third Beatitude is "Blessed are the meek, for they shall inherit the earth" (Matthew 5:5). In Genesis 12:1, the Lord promised Abram a land for possession, which was never retained by Israel. Jesus merited the true Promised Land for His people through His impoverishment on the cross. According to 2 Corinthians 5:17, how do Christians inherit the earth? According to Matthew 25:34, when will the full inheritance occur?

4. The fourth Beatitude is "Blessed are those who hunger and thirst for righteousness, for they shall be satisfied" (Matthew 5:6). Jesus' great love for us manifested itself in a hunger and thirst to acquire righteousness for us. When He was baptized, He identified Himself with sinners to "fulfill all righteousness" (Matthew 3:15). Righteousness is what God has done for us in Christ. He has justified us, that is, declared us righteous. See Romans 4:24–25. When was that hunger and thirst for righteousness fulfilled?

5. The fifth Beatitude is "Blessed are the merciful, for they shall receive mercy" (Matthew 5:7). Jesus bore the sins of the world on the cross, and when He cried out, "My God, My God, why have You forsaken Me?" (Matthew 27:46), He was asking for His Father's mercy. The Father was merciful by raising His Son from the dead. According to Matthew 18:23–27, how does Jesus act mercifully to us?

6. The sixth Beatitude is "Blessed are the pure in heart, for they shall see God" (Matthew 5:8). Pure in heart means completely committed to God with complete integrity. Jesus is truly the only one who loved the Lord with all His heart and mind and strength. He also is the only one who can see God face-to-face, as John 1:18 says. According to 1 John 1:5–10, how does Jesus make us pure in heart? According to John 14:9, how can we see God's face?

7. The seventh Beatitude is "Blessed are the peacemakers, for they shall be called sons of God" (Matthew 5:9). Jesus is identified as a peacemaker in the Messianic prophecy of Isaiah 9:6, when He is called "Prince of Peace." In His Baptism, Jesus fulfilled all righteousness and was called "Son of God." According to Romans 5:1 and Colossians 1:19–20, how does God make peace with us? When are we made sons of God?

8. The eighth Beatitude is "Blessed are those who are persecuted for righteousness' sake, for theirs is the kingdom of heaven" (Matthew 5:10). Jesus exemplifies suffering for righteousness' sake. His work is what merited the kingdom of heaven for us. Who identifies Jesus as the "Righteous One" in Matthew 27:15–20? Who should have died instead of Jesus? According to 1 Peter 2:21–25, in what manner did Jesus endure this persecution? According to 1 Peter 3:18, what was His purpose for enduring this?

3 We Live

The ninth Beatitude is "Blessed are you when others revile you and persecute you and utter all kinds of evil against you falsely on My account. Rejoice and be glad, for your reward is great in heaven, for so they persecuted the prophets who were before you" (Matthew 5:11–12). This Beatitude is different from the others. The "they" of the first eight is now replaced with "you and Me," that is, Jesus' disciple and Jesus Himself.

1. What kinds of things do you normally think of as blessings? What are typical emotions and experiences brought about by persecution? How does Jesus turn everything upside down (or right side up) in the ninth Beatitude? How did the apostles in Acts 5:40–42 live out this Beatitude? Should the absence of persecution in the life of a Christian be cause for alarm? When we are given the opportunity to suffer for the name of Jesus, how should we receive it, according to 1 Peter 4:13?

4 Closing

Family Connections

Go over your child's Growing in Christ leaflet together, each of you sharing what you learned about today's Bible story.

In Luther's Explanation to the Second Article of the Creed, he describes what Jesus has done for each of us and the fruits of His justifying work in our lives. Use the Second Article in your family devotions this week, emphasizing the righteousness that Jesus won for us through His holy blood.

Personal Reflection

The Beatitudes apply first to Jesus and then to the Church—to all believers. We cannot drive a wedge between the life of Jesus and the life of the Church, for the Church will always be conformed to the life, death, and resurrection of our Lord. This week, include the Beatitudes in your daily devotions, and reflect on all that Jesus has done for you in fulfilling them.

For Next Week

Today, we returned to the Epiphany theme of Jesus' revelation of Himself. In the Beatitudes, we see His glory in a more subtle way than in His various miracles. He teaches how He will live a life of complete humility and service in order to fulfill the demands of God's Law on our behalf. This is not glorious in the eyes of the world, but for those of us who feel the weight of sin, we find Jesus' active obedience of the Law in our place to be true glory. Next week, we will end the bright season of Epiphany as we study Jesus' Transfiguration. On the Mount of Transfiguration, God showed that His Son, Jesus, is the fulfillment of the Law and the Prophets and declared that we should listen to Him, our Savior. Read Luke 9:28–38 and 2 Peter 1:16–18.

The Transfiguration
Luke 9:28–36

Key Point

On the Mount of Transfiguration, God showed that His Son, Jesus, is the fulfillment of the Law and the Prophets and declared that we should listen to Jesus, our Savior.

Law/Gospel Points

God established the law to show/tell me what He expects of me. **God gave me His Son, who alone could do all that God expects in the Law.**

Because of my sinfulness, I cannot keep the Law of God; God chose prophets to preach sin and repentance. **God's prophets pointed to Jesus, the promised Savior who kept the Law for me.**

In my sinfulness, I think I can please God and do His will. God tells me to listen to Jesus. **God provided His Son, who alone could please God and do His will for me. God provides the Holy Spirit, who works through His Word so I can hear His message of salvation through the ears of faith.**

Connections

Bible Words
For the law was given through Moses; grace and truth came through Jesus Christ. John 1:17

Faith Words
Transfiguration, fulfillment, divine, begotten

Hymn
How Sweet the Name of Jesus Sounds (*LSB* 524; *LW* 279; *TLH* 364)

Catechism
Apostles' Creed: Second Article

Liturgy
Liturgical Colors: White

1 Opening

"Far be it from me to boast except in the cross of our Lord Jesus Christ, by which the world has been crucified to me, and I to the world," wrote St. Paul in Galatians 6:14. In 1 Corinthians 1:23, he wrote, "We preach Christ crucified." Martin Luther once said, "The cross alone is our theology." To the cross, to the cross, to the cross we go as we begin our Lenten journey this coming Ash Wednesday. Today, we are still celebrating Jesus' epiphanies, but our vantage point from the Mount of Transfiguration provides a view toward Mount Calvary, as Jesus discusses His exodus with Moses and Elijah.

1. In order to set the stage for our study of the transfiguration, read Luke 9:18–27. Based on the prophecy in Isaiah 53 that the Christ would be the Lord's Suffering Servant, how is the suffering and death of Jesus alluded to in 9:18–20? According to 9:21–22, what is the ultimate mission of the Son of Man? How does 9:23–27 indicate that the Christian life will not consist of a string of unbroken glorious times? How does a Christian take up his cross daily and follow Jesus?

2 God Speaks

The Transfiguration
Luke 9:28–36

Law
Like Peter, I do not always understand Jesus' ways and purpose. We want the glory without the cross.

Gospel
God gave me His Son, who alone could do all God demands in His Law. God provides the Holy Spirit, who works through His Word so I can hear His message of salvation through the ears of faith.

Context
This event serves as the climax of the Epiphany season. Chronologically this event occurs toward the end of Jesus' Galilean ministry. It sets up the coming Passion (Luke 9:22) as Jesus "set[s] His face to go to Jerusalem" (Luke 9:51).

Commentary

The transfiguration occurs after Peter has confessed Jesus to be the Christ (Luke 9:20). Jesus has responded by predicting His crucifixion (Luke 9:22). This is the proper order in the kingdom of God—first comes suffering, then glory.

According to Luke, the transfiguration happens about eight days after Peter's confession (Luke 9:28). This is the eighth-day theology of the Bible. God created all things in six days and rested on the seventh. The new world began on the eighth day. Male children were circumcised on the eighth day (Leviticus 12:3), a type of Baptism. Jesus rose from the dead on the eighth day, beginning a new era of grace into which we enter by Baptism.

Jesus goes up into a mountain to pray, something He often did (Luke 6:12). This time, He takes with Him the inner circle—Peter, James, and John. Suddenly, His appearance changes. This recalls the transformation of Moses after he had gone up on the mountain to be with God (Exodus 34:29). Jesus' clothes were gleaming. The same word is used of the two angels who stood guard at the empty tomb (Luke 24:4).

In the Old Testament, a truth could not be established except by the testimony of two or three witnesses. In the New Testament, we have two angels as witnesses of the resurrection (Luke 24:4) and the ascension (Acts 1:10). Here we have two witnesses from eternity, Moses and Elijah (Luke 9:30). Peter, James, and John are also there, as Peter himself would later testify: "We were eyewitnesses of His majesty" (2 Peter 1:16). The Greek word translated "departure" (ESV) in Luke 9:31 actually is *exodos*, from *ex* ("out") and *hodos* ("way"). Thus the greatest Old Testament event becomes a type and shadow of something far more important—the greatest New Testament event—the death and resurrection of our Lord, which brings deliverance not just to the Jews but to everyone in the whole world.

There is another layer of meaning here. Moses represents the Law, and Elijah represents the prophets of the Old Testament. They are speaking with Jesus about the exodus, which He is soon to accomplish in Jerusalem (Luke 9:31). In this dialogue, we find all Scripture agreeing that the death, resurrection, and ascension of Jesus is the central redemptive event in the history of the world.

When the disciples notice that Moses and Elijah are departing, the always impulsive Peter blurts out a plan to stay there. Luke notes that he didn't know what he was saying. Commentary author Arthur Just observes that at this point Peter is a true theologian of glory, wanting to avoid the cross (Matthew 16:21–23). In the kingdom of Christ, the cross comes before the crown.

Now a cloud gathers about them. This is the presence of God (Exodus 13; 40); the disciples are afraid to enter it. But there they hear the voice of God saying, "This is My Son, My Chosen One" (Luke 9:35). These words recall the words of blessing and acceptance God spoke over Jesus at His Baptism (Luke 3:22). We hear Him gladly, for He has the words of eternal life.

Discussion questions

1. The transfiguration story is filled with references and allusions to the Old Testament. Luke 9:29 describes Jesus' physical transfiguration, when "the appearance of his face was altered, and His clothing became dazzling white." Read Exodus 34:29–35. Who else's face shone with divine glory—the glory of God? Where did this person go to meet with God? Luke 9:34–35 describes a cloud overshadowing the group, and the Father's voice coming from the cloud. Read Exodus 24:12, 15–18. Who is involved in this story, and what does the cloud on the mountain represent? In Luke 1:76–79, how was the bright glory of Jesus foretold in the prophecy of John's father, Zechariah?

2. Moses and Elijah are the only two Old Testament figures who spoke with God on Mount Sinai. There are similarities between Moses and Elijah and Jesus, but the New Testament is emphatic in portraying Jesus as the fulfillment of the Law and Prophets—one greater than any prophet. As we saw in the previous question, Jesus is presented as the new Moses, who stands in God's presence and speaks on His behalf. In Luke 9:35, Jesus is called "My Son, My Chosen One," which are words that echo His Baptism in the Jordan. Neither Moses nor Elijah was ever called the "Son of God" or the "Chosen One." In Luke 9:36, the disciples see that after all the excitement, "Jesus was found alone." What could this tell us about the importance of Jesus in relation to Moses and Elijah? In John 1:14–17, to what could "we have seen His glory" refer? How does John depict the relationship between Moses and Jesus?

3. As we have noted, the Greek word translated as "departure" in Luke 9:31 is actually *exodos* or *Exodus*. According to Psalm 78:51–55, what did God do for His people in the exodus? Based on Exodus 19:1–6, how do you think the exodus provided the basis for all the future promises of God? What do the Old Testament exodus and the New Testament one of Jesus' death, resurrection, and ascension have in common?

4. We have already noted how the reference to Jesus' exodus pointed to His passion, death, and resurrection. There are a number of other similarities and contrasts between the transfiguration and Jesus' crucifixion. Read Luke 23:32–43, and identify some of these similarities and contrasts.

5. In Luke 24:4, the two angels at the empty tomb are there in "dazzling apparel," using language similar to Jesus' appearance at the transfiguration. This suggests a connection between the divine glory of Jesus shown in the transfiguration and of His subsequent glorification shown by the resurrection. It also points forward to the glory that we will share with Him when we are raised from the dead on the Last Day. What connection is there between Luke 24:44–47 and the transfiguration account?

3 We Live

1. Have you ever wondered what people talk about in heaven? Based on our lesson today, what do you think they talk about? What does this fact about heaven teach us about our lives here on earth?

2. What do we find Jesus doing in Luke 3:21–22 and 9:18–20? According to Luke 9:28, for what reason did Jesus go up on the mountain? What does this tells us about the transfiguration account? How could Jesus' example apply to our own lives?

3. In Luke 9:35, the Father declares from heaven, "This is My Son, My Chosen One; listen to Him!" Read Deuteronomy 18:15–19. How does this passage from Moses shed light on the words of the Father at the transfiguration? The last part of the Father's statement actually could be translated, "Continue always to listen to Him!" According to 2 Peter 1:16–21, who provided an eyewitness account of this event, and how can we continue to listen to Jesus?

4 Closing

Family Connections

Go over your child's Growing in Christ leaflet together, each of you sharing what you learned about today's Bible story.

Also continue to study the Second Article in the Small Catechism. If your family has memorized the Second Article, you might try adding the First and Third Articles too. The First Article speaks of the Father of Jesus, who gives everything to us out of sheer mercy. The Third Article confesses the Holy Spirit, who delivers forgiveness to us in the Church and will transfigure our bodies on the Last Day when we are raised from the dead.

Personal Reflection

It's hard to imagine a sharper contrast between the glorious and bright end of Epiphany and the darker days of Lent. The Transfiguration of Our Lord is always celebrated on the Last Sunday after the Epiphany, which is the last Sunday before Lent begins.

Although at first glance Transfiguration and Ash Wednesday seem to clash, the transfiguration of Jesus actually provides a wonderful segue into Lent. We, like Peter ("Lord, it is good for us to be here."), desire to stay in

Epiphany where things are glorious and bright, celebrating the glory of Christ's divinity. We like to see the miraculous Jesus, not the Suffering Servant. But if Jesus had stopped with Epiphany, He would have stopped short of our salvation.

From the Mount of Transfiguration, Jesus can see clearly where He is going. He knows that His is the way of the cross. Jesus was discussing His exodus, His bloody departure, with Moses and Elijah. The voice of the Father booms, "This is My Son, My Chosen One!" These words connect us back to Jesus' Baptism, where He took upon Himself the sin of the world, and connect us forward to Jesus' sacrificial death for sin.

God the Father tells the disciples, "Listen to Him!" What does Jesus then say in their hearing? According to Matthew, He says, "Don't be afraid." There is nothing to fear. Jesus will win salvation on the cross. He says, "Tell no one the vision, until the Son of Man is raised from the dead" (Matthew 17:9). This prediction of His resurrection assures them that God's glory will again be revealed, but this time, it will be for good!

Matthew tells us that on the Mount of Transfiguration, the disciples couldn't bear the unveiled presence of God. God has graciously hidden Himself in the man Jesus so that we may face Him without fear. As Peter, James, and John looked up and "Jesus was found alone," let us look to no one else during Lent. Although repentant fasting and bodily preparation are fine practices during Lent, our primary focus should always be on Jesus' saving work on the cross.

The Lenten Gradual, based on Hebrews 12:2, provides us with the perfect Lenten theme: "Oh come, let us fix our eyes on Jesus, the author and perfecter of our faith, who for the joy set before him endured the cross, scorning its shame, and sat down at the right hand of the throne of God." Amen!

For Next Week

This week, we saw the final Epiphany revelation of Jesus' glory. As we enter Lent, we will focus on Jesus' journey to the cross and on His active obedience of God's Law in our place. Next week, we will study the temptation of Jesus by Satan. The devil tried and tried to seduce Jesus into giving up His focus on the cross and replace it with the glory of instant gratification. Because of our Lord's triumph over Satan—in the desert and on the cross—God forgives the repentant sinner who has given in to Satan's wiles. To prepare for next week, read Luke 4:1–13.

The Temptation of Jesus

Luke 4:1–13

Key Point

Like us, Jesus was tempted by Satan to sin. Yet, for us, He overcame all temptation because we cannot.

Law/Gospel Points

God wants me to trust Him and not test His love and care for me. **In spite of my sinful ways that place me in harm, God watches over and protects me with His holy angels.**

Connections

Bible Words

For we do not have a high priest who is unable to sympathize with our weaknesses, but one who in every respect has been tempted as we are, yet without sin. Hebrews 4:15

Faith Words

Lent, temptation, resist, High Priest

Hymn

Christ, the Lord of Hosts, Unshaken (*LSB* 521)

Catechism

Lord's Prayer: Sixth and Seventh Petitions

Liturgy

Clergy Vestments

1 Opening

1. Hebrews 4:15 says that Jesus "in every respect has been tempted as we are, yet without sin." Though it is possible for us to face a temptation without sinning, to what does the experience of temptation usually lead?

2. We learn in Jesus' Baptism in Luke 3:21–23 that He is the Son of God. This is reiterated in His genealogy, but Luke 3:38 also calls Him "the son of Adam." As we reflect on the fact that Jesus was both true God and true Man, what are we tempted to conclude about His temptation by Satan?

3. In this lesson, we see Jesus resist Satan by relying on the Word of God alone. He used no miracles, divine power, or deep theological insights. He overcame the devil by quoting the Book of Deuteronomy three times. What might this tempt us to identify as the main point of the story?

2 God Speaks

The Temptation of Jesus
Luke 4:1–13

Law
We often succumb to the devil's temptation to get glory now and avoid the cross.

Gospel
Jesus defeats Satan and wins salvation for us.

Context

This event occurs immediately after Jesus' Baptism and marks the beginning of His ministry. While out of order chronologically, this is the traditional text for the First Sunday in Lent, when we focus on the suffering Savior.

Commentary

In this account, Jesus is "full of the Holy Spirit," having just been baptized (Luke 3:21–22). The Holy Spirit leads our Savior not to glory but to suffering. Jesus goes about His saving work through His active obedience. The glory will follow. Jesus is in the desert, the place of chaos and sterility as opposed to Paradise, the place of fertility and order (Genesis 2). Jesus is there for forty days. This immediately recalls the wanderings of Israel in the desert for forty years (Deuteronomy 8:2) and the fasting of Moses on Sinai (Exodus 24:18).

Jesus is tempted by the devil. The Greek word *diabolos* ("devil," like the Spanish *Diablo*) means "slanderer" or "accuser." The devil always accuses us before the judgment seat of God. But Christ is our advocate who pleads for us, offering His own blood in expiation of our guilt. This passage contrasts Adam with Christ, who is the last Adam. Adam began in Paradise, was tempted, fell, and went from life to death. Jesus began in the desert, was tempted but overcame, and went from death to life.

There are three temptations. Each centers on and challenges the identity of Jesus—which Satan well knows—as the Son of God. Luke has established that Jesus is the Son of God in his accounts of the Baptism (Luke 3:22) and the genealogy (Luke 3:38), which immediately precede this passage. To each temptation, Jesus responds with the written Word of God, all quotes from Deuteronomy.

Jesus is hungry after fasting for forty days. Satan tempts Him not only to feed Himself, but also to become a bread king, appealing to men's most base desires. Jesus cites Deuteronomy 8:3: "Man does not live by bread alone." Matthew adds that we live spiritually by the Word of God. Having overcome this temptation, Jesus is qualified to feed men's bodies with bread, as in the feeding of the five thousand, and to feed their souls with the bread of life through Holy Communion (Matthew 26:26).

Next, Satan claims to have authority over the kingdoms of this world, and he will give those kingdoms to Jesus if Jesus worships him. Satan is lying. He is king only over sinners and not a complete ruler even at that, as Luther shows in *Bondage of the Will*. We soon see in Luke that Jesus has true divine authority in His teaching (Luke 4:32) and in His miracles (Luke 4:36). Jesus counters by citing Deuteronomy 6:13, "You shall worship the Lord your God, and Him only shall you serve" (Luke 4:8). Jesus is, of course, the Second

Person of the Holy Trinity and worthy of worship Himself. Indeed, at the name of Jesus every knee shall bow (Philippians 2:10), including the devil's.

Satan, in the last temptation, quotes, or rather misquotes, Scripture himself citing Psalm 91:11–12. Seeing that the devil can twist Scripture, we cannot be too careful about pure doctrine. The devil here, as in all temptations, wants Jesus—and us in our Christian life—to bypass the cross and go straight to the glory. But Jesus quotes Deuteronomy 6:16 and defeats the devil by telling him not to tempt God. Jesus Christ Himself is God—God who suffers and dies for you and me.

Discussion questions

1. According to Matthew 3:13–15, why did Jesus come to be baptized by John? What does Jesus' obedience under temptation do for us? What does Jesus' obedience even to death on the cross do for us?

2. We noted above some of the Old Testament themes that appear in the account of Jesus' temptation. In Genesis 2:16–17, God gave Adam permission to eat from any tree in the Garden of Eden except for the tree of the knowledge of good and evil. According to Genesis 3:1–3, what did Satan tempt Eve to do? In what way did she fail to respond properly? According to Exodus 17:1–7, how did the children of Israel tempt or test God in the wilderness? What is the significance of the location Massah and Meribah?

3. With regard to the first temptation, we know Jesus had received confirmation of His Sonship at His Baptism. According to Luke 4:3, how does Satan challenge that Sonship? Jesus' response in Luke 4:4 is a quotation from Deuteronomy 8:1–3. Why could Jesus confidently rely on His Father to provide for Him?

4. With regard to the second temptation, Isaiah 52–53 tells us that Jesus will be the servant of the Lord who will suffer for the people but then be exalted. In Luke 4:5–7, what does Satan tempt Jesus to do? According to Luke 22:39–44, what struggle did Jesus continue to face? Jesus responds to Satan by quoting Deuteronomy 6:13. According to Deuteronomy 6:10–15, what provides the basis for serving the Lord God only?

5. Finally, we see the third temptation. "The devil can cite Scripture for his purpose," wrote Shakespeare in *The Merchant of Venice*. In Luke 4:9–11, Satan rips Scripture verses out of context and makes himself sound very pious. After forty days of suffering in the wilderness, Jesus could have been aching for an external sign that His Father had not abandoned Him. Yet Jesus knew the background of Deuteronomy 6:16. In this verse, what is the significance of Massah for Jesus' temptation? (Refer back to question 2.) According to Luke 4:13, what did Satan do after being defeated this time?

3 We Live

1. In Satan's first temptation of Jesus, he tempts Him to despair of God's mercy. What is despair, why is it dangerous, and how can it be overcome?

2. In the second temptation, Satan tempts Jesus toward an apparent good. Jesus came into the world to be a ruler, so why not just start now by worshiping the devil? What are some seemingly good things that tempt us? How does Jesus tell good from evil?

3. In the third temptation, Satan tempts Jesus by misusing God's Word. He quotes out of context. This happens a great deal today. Consider the following paraphrases of Scripture, and provide examples of contemporary misuses of them: "Forgive others," "Do not judge," "God is love." How does Jesus resist this temptation?

4. How does what happens to Jesus after His Baptism relate to our Christian life? According to 1 Peter 5:8–9, what expectation should a new Christian have after Baptism? Who is Satan most interested in tempting? What is Satan's ultimate goal? What is our best defense against Satan?

4 Closing

Family Connections

Go over your child's Growing in Christ leaflet together, each of you sharing what you learned about today's Bible story.

In the Small Catechism, Luther provides helpful insight into our source of defense against the devil. In the explanation to the Sixth Petition of the Lord's Prayer, Luther says that we pray in order to petition God for protection from "the devil, the world, and our sinful nature." This unholy trinity is constantly seeking to "deceive us or mislead us into false belief, despair, and other great shame and vice." The help we are to continually pray for is "that we may finally overcome them and win the victory."

In a similar way, the Seventh Petition is directed toward constant protection from the evil one, Satan. It also is oriented toward our last hour, when we will need the Lord's protection for a blessed end.

We also can look to the Creed for the answers to our prayers. In the explanation of the First Article, we confess, "I believe that God . . . defends me against all danger and guards and protects me from all evil." In the Second Article, he writes, "I believe that Jesus Christ . . . has redeemed me, a lost and condemned person, purchased and won me from all sins, from death, and from the power of the devil."

This week, study the Sixth and Seventh Petitions with your family and work on memorizing them. These will help us all remember the daily need to come before the Lord in prayer.

Personal Reflection

Luther sees the trio of the devil, the world, and our sinful nature as the source of all temptations to sin. In the Large Catechism, Luther expounds on those three tempters and urges us to pray.

First, the sinful nature:

Exerts himself and encourages us daily into unchastity, laziness, gluttony and drunkenness, greed and deception, to defraud our neighbor and to overcharge him. In short, the old Adam encourages us to have all kinds of evil lusts, which cling to us by nature and to which we are moved by the society, the example, and what we hear and see of other people. They often wound and inflame even an innocent heart.

Next comes the world, which offends us in word and deed. It drives us to anger and impatience. In short, there is nothing but hatred and envy, hostility, violence and wrong, unfaithfulness, vengeance, cursing, railing, slander, pride and haughtiness, with useless finery, honor, fame, and power. Everyone desires to sit at the head of the group and to be seen before all.

Then comes the devil, pushing and provoking in all directions. But he especially agitates matters that concern the conscience and spiritual affairs. He leads us to despise and disregard both God's Word and works. He tears us away from faith, hope, and love, and he brings us into misbelief, false security, and stubbornness. Or, on the other hand, he leads us to despair, denial of God, blasphemy, and innumerable other shocking things. These are snares and nets, indeed, real fiery darts that are shot like poison into the heart, not by flesh and blood, but by the devil" (LC III 102–04).

The intensity of the attacks upon us are so great that "We are moved to cry out and to pray that God would not allow us to become weary and faint and to fall again into sin, shame, and unbelief. For otherwise it is impossible to overcome even the least temptation" (LC III 105).

This week, reflect on the persistence of Satan's attacks, and pray fervently for deliverance from his wiles. But more importantly, reflect on the fact that Jesus has defeated Satan. As we cling to Christ in faith, Satan cannot harm us!

Adult Leader Guide

Lesson 1

The Birth of John Foretold
Luke 1:5–25

Opening

Open class with a prayer tied to the **Key Point** for the lesson. For example, this week's prayer could be: "Lord God, in Your mercy, You promised to send John to prepare sinful people for the coming of Your Son. Continue to send preachers of Your Word to call us to repentance and declare us righteous for the sake of Jesus' suffering, death, and resurrection. In His name we pray. Amen." After the prayer, sing or say the hymn(s) together. Then read the Bible lesson, review introductory material, and begin the opening questions.

1. Jesus' first advent was in the incarnation, when He took the flesh of the Virgin Mary, lived a blameless life in our place, suffered, died, and rose again for our salvation. After His ascension, He did not really leave us but is only hidden from our sight. He promised to be with the Church until the end of time. He will be where two or three are gathered in His Name, in the preaching of the Gospel, in Baptism, and in His body and blood. Anywhere the Word is preached faithfully and the Sacraments are given out according to His institution, an advent of Jesus occurs. That is, He comes to forgive and comfort us, so every Sunday is a little Advent. Jesus' final advent will occur on the Last Day, when He returns to judge the living and the dead. Advent is the time in the Church Year when we remember Jesus' coming in the incarnation, we celebrate His presence among us in Word and Sacrament, and we look forward to His return to take us to be with Him in heaven.

2. Often the Old Testament sacrifices and rites seem strange to us. Yet God promised to work through the temple in order to cleanse and sanctify His people. Many of the rites were rich in symbolic value. In Psalm 141:2, the psalmist prays to the Lord, "Let my prayer be counted as incense before You, and the lifting up of my hands as the evening sacrifice!" Incense and the lifting up of hands are closely associated with prayer. Incense rises up, and similarly, our prayers ascend to God. As we lift our hands to the Lord, we show our faith in Him and pray for His mercy. The rites and symbols of Old Testament worship were visible reminders of the believer's posture before God. The prayers of the worshipper were combined with tangible actions. Worship was physical as well as spiritual. Though most Lutherans do not use incense in worship, we do use many signs and actions that reflect our posture

before God. For example, standing and kneeling are special postures for prayer, and the sign of the cross is often made in remembrance of our Baptism.

3. The word *apostle* means "one who is sent" with a message to deliver or an action to perform. The apostles were sent out by Jesus to proclaim the Gospel, baptize, celebrate the Lord's Supper, and establish churches everywhere they were sent. The apostles set apart pastors, such as Timothy and Titus, in the places where they established churches to serve as Christ's messengers. Yet all Christians serve as witnesses of Christ, since each is called to be "prepared to make a defense to anyone who asks you for a reason for the hope that is in you" (1 Peter 3:15). We can tell which messengers are true ones by comparing their message to God's inspired and inerrant Word, the Bible.

God Speaks

1. Paul tells us in Romans 3:23 that "all have sinned and fall short of the glory of God." This "all" means that Zechariah, Elizabeth, and all other people are sinful and cannot stand innocent before God's judgment. Yet Romans 3:24 goes on to tell us that all "are justified [declared righteous] by His grace as a gift, through the redemption that is in Christ Jesus." This gift excludes the possibility of works contributing to salvation. Rather, God has declared everyone not guilty in Christ Jesus. Zechariah and Elizabeth believed in God's promise to send a Messiah to save them from their sins, and God counted their faith as righteousness before Him. This is what it means when we speak of justification by faith. God promises salvation to the world through Jesus, and whoever believes and is baptized will be saved. Of course, God does allow people to reject His gifts. When Luke tells us that Zechariah and Elizabeth were "walking blamelessly in all the commandments and statutes of the Lord" (Luke 1:6), this means that they followed the external requirements of the Old Testament Law blamelessly, but this does not mean they were sinless.

2. The story of Abraham and Sarah is very similar to the story of Zechariah and Elizabeth. In Abraham's case, God Himself speaks to him and promises a son to be born in the couple's old age. Abraham falls on his face laughing at this idea. Later, in Genesis 18:9–15, Sarah also shows her doubt in the promise by laughing. Zechariah's response is equally unfaithful. He doubts that God can provide a child to such an old couple and asks for a sign from Gabriel as proof. What is comforting about both of these stories is that they demonstrate God's patience and forgiveness for His saints. Even the people the Bible calls "righteous" were at the same time sinners who had doubts that

vex and plague God's people even today. God never makes excuses for their sin (as He doesn't for ours), nor makes light of their unbelief. Yet He graciously forgives the guilt of their sin and unbelief and restores them to faith, which is what He still does through His Church today.

3. The key phrases in Malachi are: "Behold, I will send you Elijah the prophet . . . he will turn the hearts of fathers to their children" (4:5–6). The key phrases in Luke: "in the spirit and power of Elijah, to turn the hearts of the fathers to the children" (Luke 1:17). We see in these phrases that God's prophecy to send a great prophet like Elijah would come true in John's ministry. John was the prophet who would come to prepare the people for "the great and awesome day of the Lord." That day arrived in the person of Jesus Christ of Nazareth.

4. John "went into all the region around the Jordan, proclaiming a baptism of repentance for the forgiveness of sins" (Luke 3:3). John's basic message was a call to the people to turn away from their sins and find forgiveness from the Lord in his Baptism of repentance. (John's Baptism did forgive sins, but it was not exactly the same as Christian Baptism, since Jesus had not yet died and risen again or sent His Holy Spirit.) Luke 1:16 says that many children of Israel will return to the Lord by responding to John's message. Yet Luke 1:17 says that he will "turn the hearts of the fathers to the children, and the disobedient to the wisdom of the just." One of Luke's major themes is to describe how God's covenant with Israel is fulfilled in Christ and how a New Testament is set in place that is intended not just for the children of Israel but also for Gentiles. John's job is to prepare for Christ's coming, which includes calling the children of Israel to repentance and also showing them that the doors are opening to include all people. In Luke 1:17, the "fathers" are the children of Israel and the "children" are the Gentiles. John's preaching will open the hearts of the fathers to see that the time is at hand for the children to become heirs of God's grace. Through John's preaching, some of the Gentiles will repent and believe, that is, "the disobedient" will turn "to the wisdom of the just."

5. Numbers 6:2 says that a person takes the Nazirite vow "to separate himself to the LORD." The Nazirite would avoid the fruit of the vine (wine) and take other steps to show that he was set apart for the Lord's use. Earthly pleasures were not to get in the way of the Nazirite's focus on the Lord. John was the last of the Old Testament prophets, and his Nazarite vow set the stage for his somber and austere preaching in the desert. His message was one of

repentance in preparation for Jesus' arrival. The time of rejoicing had not quite come. Psalm 104:14–15 praises God because He causes "the grass to grow for the livestock and plants for man to cultivate, that he may bring forth food from the earth and wine to gladden the heart of man, oil to make his face shine and bread to strengthen man's heart." Wine is a sign of joy and gladness. Consider the festivity of the wedding at Cana (John 2:1–11). Jesus, like John, preached repentance, but He also pointed to Himself and said, "The kingdom of heaven is at hand." In other words, Jesus proclaimed that the time of God's favor had arrived, so rejoicing had a perfectly appropriate place in His ministry. Today, He continues to give us the gift of wine for rejoicing—in moderation, of course! But even better, He gives us His own blood of the New Testament in the Lord's Supper in, with, and under wine for the forgiveness of our sins.

We Live

1. Misfortunes occur in our lives for so many reasons that we should never seek to interpret them as signs of God's punishment. We know that He loves us because of His Son's sacrifice for us. It is true that "the Lord disciplines the one he loves" (Hebrews 12:6). Every difficult trial is an occasion for repentance. Whenever we are suffering, we should look to the Word and Sacraments for comfort and strength. God tenderly invites us to pray for His help. Many people today seek to confirm God's love for them through outward signs, like health, wealth, and success. God would not have us rely on such transitory things but on His Word, which endures forever.

2. Only the Holy Spirit can give faith, and He works through the Word and Sacraments. Though these passages cannot give us absolute certainty about the possibility of unborn children today receiving faith through the Word, they strongly suggest it. It is very clear from these passages that unborn children were valued highly and were loved by their parents. Infants who are baptized according to Christ's command (Matthew 28:19) have all the precious promises that Baptism gives, including forgiveness, life, and salvation, all of which the Holy Spirit works through faith. Such examples from Scripture remind us to continue to speak out against abortion, support laws against it, and offer assistance to organizations that work to prevent women from having abortions.

Closing

Encourage the adults with children in Sunday School to review their child's Growing in Christ Leaflet together at home.

For the **Family Connections** section, encourage the class to study the Small Catechism at home regularly, especially if they have children. Children are able to memorize well, and the catechism will be a great asset for them throughout their lives. If students in the class do not have catechisms for themselves and their children, see if the church has copies available for distribution.

Lesson 2

The Birth of Jesus Foretold
Luke 1:26–38

Opening

Open class with a prayer tied to the **Key Point** for the lesson. For example, this week's prayer might be: "Lord God, You found favor with Mary by grace alone and chose her to be the mother of Your Son. Look with favor on us, we pray, for the sake of Jesus Christ, who was born of the Virgin for us men and for our salvation. In His name we pray. Amen." After the prayer, sing or say the hymn(s) together. Then read the Bible lesson, review introductory material, and begin the opening questions.

1. Since the time of the Enlightenment in the eighteenth century, it has been commonly thought that the virgin birth and other miracles in the Bible could not have happened since they contradict laws of nature or human reason. Some people have attempted to retain the Christian faith while embracing such modernistic ideas, but at great harm to themselves and the Church. There are several reasons that we must confess the virgin birth clearly. The first reason is that God's Word, the Bible, confesses it. Isaiah 7:14 specifically says that the Messiah will be born of a virgin, and this verse is quoted in Matthew 1:23. Matthew 1:25 makes it clear that Joseph and Mary did not have sexual intercourse until she had given birth, and Luke 1:26–38 testifies that Mary was a virgin when she conceived. The second reason we must maintain the virgin birth is that if Jesus had two human parents, He would have been born with sin. Only by virtue of the fact that He is the Son of God is He sinless and able to save us from our sins.

2. "Nothing will be impossible with God" could be misused by Christians who say things like, "If you just believe enough, God will heal your cancer, since nothing is impossible for Him." While it is true that God can still perform miracles of healing, He has not promised to do so. The statement of Gabriel applies to God's ability to make Elizabeth fertile in her old age and Mary pregnant without relations with a man. We should apply this verse today when people cast doubt on God's ability to perform the things the Bible claims He can do, such as creating out of nothing, forgiving sins through His Word, saving people through Baptism, and making Jesus' body and blood present in, with, and under bread and wine.

3. Luke 1:35 states that Jesus will be called "the Son of God." In the Nicene Creed, we confess that Jesus Christ is "the only-begotten Son of God, begotten of His Father before all worlds, God of God, Light of Light, Very God of Very God, begotten, not made, being of one substance with the Father, by whom all things were made." Since Jesus is fully God and fully man, and He was born of the Virgin Mary, then we can (and should) say that Mary is the mother of God. In the Early Church, several notorious heretics refused to give Mary the title "mother of God" because they were trying to separate Jesus' divine and human natures. Of course, this phrase can be misunderstood to mean that Mary existed before God, which is preposterous. But properly understood, calling Mary the "mother of God" is a bold confession that her Son is true God and true man in one person. (Note: The title "mother of God" appears in the Lutheran Confessions, both in the Formula of Concord Epitome VIII 12 and Solid Declaration VIII 24.)

4. The Annunciation is celebrated on March 25, nine months before Christmas Day. Some congregations have a Divine Service on this day and celebrate a little bit of Advent in March.

God Speaks

1. In Luke 1:18, Zechariah asks, "How shall I know this?" In other words, he wanted a sign to prove that the birth would take place; the Word from Gabriel wasn't enough. On the other hand, Mary asks, "How will this be, since I am a virgin?" She does not question the possibility of the miraculous birth happening but simply asks *how* it will happen. Zechariah's words belied unbelief; Mary's words represented genuine astonishment, not unbelief. She took the Lord's Word on it. "Behold, I am the servant of the Lord; let it be to me according to your word" (Luke 1:38). We learn from this comparison that the proper response to a promise from God is to believe it, which is none other than faith. What God says He will do, He does. His Word is sure and dependable. The promises you have received in the Gospel, Absolution, Baptism, and the Lord's Supper are unshakeable.

2. *Favor* is another word for grace. A true favor for someone would be done without expecting anything in return. In Genesis 6:8, Moses tells us that "Noah found favor in the eyes of the LORD," but he does not say that Noah was seeking His favor. Neither was Mary seeking God's favor. She did not have any special attribute that made God favor her. Rather, by grace He decided to favor her in that she would bear the Messiah. When we talk of being justified by grace, we mean that God looks at us with favor—that is, He

is pleased with us—for the sake of Christ's sacrifice on the cross. When God looks with favor on us, it is not because of anything that we do, but solely for the sake of Christ. Ephesians 1:7, for example, says that "In [Christ] we have redemption through His blood, the forgiveness of our trespasses, according to the riches of His grace."

3. According to Matthew, Jesus' name means that He will "save His people from their sins." Many Jews were expecting a powerful and glorious Messiah, an earthly king. Matthew makes it clear that Jesus' reign would be a spiritual one, for He had come not to save a limited number of people (the Jews) from their earthly foes but to make atonement for the sins of the whole world and save them from God's condemnation of them on account of their sins. Of course, many people would reject Jesus in unbelief and remain under God's wrath.

4. 2 Samuel 7:11b says that the Lord will make a house for David; Luke 1:27 says that Jesus' stepfather Joseph was of the house of David, which is how Jesus could be considered a "son of David" (Matthew 1:1) and therefore the Messiah. In 2 Samuel 7:12–13, 16 we learn that the Lord will establish the Messiah's kingdom and throne forever; Isaiah 9:7 teaches that the Messiah will have David's throne and an everlasting kingdom; Luke 1:32–33 records that Jesus will have the throne of His father, David, and His kingdom will never end. 2 Samuel 7:14 instructs that the Lord will be the Messiah's Father, and the Messiah His Son; Luke 1:32 says that Jesus will be called "Son of the Most High" and in 1:35 that He will be called "Son of God." We see in these verses that Luke is concerned with demonstrating that Jesus is both the Messiah (Christ) and true God (Son of God).

We Live

1. In the Apostles' Creed, we confess that Jesus was "born of the Virgin Mary." In the Nicene Creed, we say that the eternal Son of God "was incarnate by the Holy Spirit of the virgin Mary." In the liturgies of Vespers and Evening Prayer, we sing the Magnificat, Mary's song from Luke 1:46–55. Mary's role is essential, for our Lord Jesus took His flesh from this faithful woman. For this reason, this humble woman will always be called blessed and worthy of respect and imitation (Luke 1:48).

2. In Baptism, all of us are born again by the Holy Spirit and are made holy sons and daughters of God. Note that in 1 Corinthians 6:11 that *sanctified* means "made holy." Jesus teaches Nicodemus of the necessity of the new

birth by the water and the Spirit in John 3:5. In Galatians 3:26–27, St. Paul teaches that all who are baptized into Christ are sons of God. Romans 8:14–17 links the Spirit to our adoption as sons of God.

3. No one will ever be near Immanuel, "God with us," in the same way Mary was. He was a little baby in her womb; yet even bearing the Son of God cannot save. Mary was saved through faith, that is, trust in God, who had come into her womb so that He could be born and atone for her sins and the sins of the world. The God made flesh is not far from us today but is still Immanuel, as He says in Matthew 28:20, "Behold, I am with you always, to the end of the age." He is with us in the preaching of His Word and the absolution of our sins through the Office of the Ministry. He is with us in Baptism, as we are united to Him. And He is with us in His body and blood to deliver forgiveness in the Sacrament of the Altar. What great cause for rejoicing!

Closing

Encourage the adults with children in Sunday School to review their child's Growing in Christ Leaflet together at home.

For the **Family Connections** section, encourage the class to study the Small Catechism at home regularly, especially if they have children. Children are able to memorize well, and the catechism will be a great asset for them throughout their lives. If students in the class do not have catechisms for themselves and their children, see if the church has copies available for distribution.

Lesson 3

The Birth of John
Luke 1:57–80

Opening

Open class with a prayer tied to the **Key Point** for the lesson. For example, this week's prayer might be: "Lord God, You spoke Your Word through Zechariah, announcing that his son, John, would give people the knowledge of salvation in the forgiveness of sins. Continue to send pastors to speak Your Word to us today, declaring us righteous for the sake of Jesus Christ and giving us the knowledge of Your great salvation. In Jesus' name. Amen."

After the prayer, sing or say the hymn(s) together. Then read the Bible lesson, review introductory material, and begin the opening questions.

1. God's Word never tells us to forgive ourselves. It tells us that God forgives the sins of repentant sinners and that we should forgive sins that others commit against us. The problem with statements like "You have to learn to forgive yourself" is that it uses theological language but infuses it with psychological meaning. In Psalm 51, David makes it clear that we stand guilty before God because of our sin, and so only His forgiveness can restore us to innocence. Our sinful nature causes guilty feelings over what we have done to linger. But as Christians, we know that God has forgiven all of our sins for Jesus' sake, and we can stand confidently before Him without fear of damnation. David would have us say, "You have to learn to find forgiveness from Jesus!"

2. God showed His grace and mercy to His people by sending John to call them to repentance in preparation for His Son's arrival. As we have seen, God's name is holy, and it sanctifies (makes holy) those things to which it is attached. This is why many people find it helpful to make the sign of the cross along with the words, "In the name of the Father and of the Son and of the Holy Spirit" in remembrance of their Baptism. With His name upon us, we are confident that we are His.

God Speaks

1. Though it is used less commonly today, a covenant is basically a contract between two parties in which both are required to perform certain actions. We must be careful not to misunderstand Old Testament covenants this way.

Certainly, some of the covenants that God made with Israel were contract-like, but the ones He made with Abraham were one-sided. That is, God was promising to follow through on whatever He promised. God gave such a covenant in Jeremiah 31:31–34. This new covenant would involve God forgiving the guilt of His people, no longer remembering their sins. In Luke 22:20, Jesus says that the cup of wine in the Lord's Supper is "the new covenant in My blood." That blood forgives our guilt, and the Lord remembers our sins no more. This is the new covenant that the Lord has made with us. Lutherans usually—and correctly—translate the phrase "New Testament" to emphasize the fact that we contribute nothing to it, but simply receive the Lord's forgiveness in faith. When you are the heir to someone's last will and testament, you do not contribute a thing.

2. Zechariah's Spirit-filled prophecy in Luke 1:68b–75 talks about what God has done for Israel in the past; Luke 1:76–79 prophesies about what God will do in the future through John the Baptist and Jesus. Luke 1:76–77 shows that John will prepare the way for Jesus by showing people salvation in the forgiveness of sins. 1:78–79 shows that John will prepare the way for the light of the world. Luke 3:4 quotes Isaiah the prophet's prediction of John's coming. Jesus identifies Himself as a prophet in Luke 4:24. He was the last and greatest of the prophets.

3. John would proclaim a Baptism of repentance for the forgiveness of sins (Luke 3:3). Jesus says that the essential message of the Church is that "repentance and forgiveness of sins should be proclaimed in his name to all nations" (Luke 24:47). Jesus' suffering, death, and resurrection provide full forgiveness of our sins and are the basis for that message (Luke 24:46). This message is so important because all of us are sinners, and if our sins are not forgiven, we cannot stand in the presence of our perfect and holy God.

4. The word *justify* means "to declare righteous." It is the language of a courtroom. One who is declared not guilty is declared righteous. That is what we try to do when we justify our own actions. That is, we declare our actions righteous and good. Romans 4:1–9 shows that when God forgives sinners, He "justifies the ungodly." He renders a verdict of not guilty, based not on our works but on Jesus' work. The Pharisee in Luke 18:9–14 thought that his personal holiness and good works were the basis for his justification before God. The tax collector knew that, as a sinner, the only way he could be justified was by having his sins forgiven. Romans 4:5 shows that "faith is counted as righteousness." By faith, we mean a simple trust in God's

forgiveness. Abraham, David, Zechariah, Elizabeth, Simeon, the tax collector, and all of us are righteous by faith. The Lord does not count our sins against us, but justifies us for Jesus' sake! And how are we justified? This is done through the preaching of the Gospel, and in Holy Absolution, Holy Baptism, and Holy Communion. These are the means that the Lord provides for justifying the ungodly.

We Live

1. Many people think that holiness is all about the purity of a person's outward works and inward thoughts. While purity or the absence of sin is an aspect of holiness, the biblical understanding of *holy* emphasizes things that are "from God" or "set apart by God." Luke 1:49 says that God's name is holy; 1:70 speaks of the "holy prophets" that God set apart to deliver His Word; 1:72 refers to the "holy covenant" with Abraham that came from God; 1:75 says that God's people served Him in holiness, set apart and special; 3:16 says that Jesus will baptize people with "the Holy Spirit," namely, God's Spirit. In Lutheran churches, we speak of the Holy Scriptures, Holy Baptism, Holy Communion, Holy Absolution, the Holy Christian Church, the Office of the Holy Ministry. All of these things are gifts from God and are set apart by Him to do the work of making us holy. We are holied by the forgiveness of sins that He gives out through those holy things.

2. The word *mercy* can be used to describe a number of concepts. We have noted before that grace is God's favorable attitude toward us. Perhaps we could say that God demonstrates His grace toward us through acts of mercy. In Luke 1:50, God's mercy is His general grace or favor. In 1:54, His mercy is seen through His faithfulness to His promises. In 1:58, His mercy is shown as the barren Elizabeth is given a son. In 1:72, God's mercy is shown in His love and faithfulness. In 1:77–78, the tender mercy of our God is found in the forgiveness of sins and Jesus. In 6:36, followers of Jesus are told to be merciful toward others, just as the Father is merciful. In 10:37, the Good Samaritan is said to have shown mercy by helping a helpless man. The followers of Jesus are told to do likewise. We see that God's mercy is shown freely and in many saving ways. Christians, being freely forgiven, can serve their neighbors by showing mercy. Our basis and example for showing mercy are in God's mercy shown through His Son. Note that in our worship services, we often ask for the Lord's mercy. In the Kyrie and other places, we pray "Lord, have mercy." Such prayers for mercy are general requests for God to continue to act graciously toward us, even as He has demonstrated His mercy to us through His Son.

3. Answers about peace will vary. In Luke 2:29–30, Simeon realizes that he can peacefully leave this world at the Lord's bidding now that his own eyes have seen His salvation in the baby Jesus, the Messiah. Simeon's peace came from the knowledge of salvation. In Luke 24:36–39, Jesus speaks peace to the disciples and provides peace by showing that He had risen from the dead. In the saving wounds of Jesus and on account of His resurrection, we know that peace between God and humankind has been achieved. With our sins forgiven, we have perfect peace.

4. Answers will vary. We should recognize that the congregation is the place where the family of God gathers to receive His gifts, and that we do have opportunities and obligations for love and service to each other. Seeking out the lonely and disconnected is an important service that Christians can do.

Closing

Encourage the adults with children in Sunday School to review their child's Growing in Christ Leaflet together at home.

For the **Family Connections** section, encourage the class to study the Small Catechism at home regularly, especially if they have children. Children are able to memorize well, and the catechism will be a great asset for them throughout their lives.

Lesson 4

The Birth of Jesus
Luke 2:1–20

Opening

Open class with a prayer tied to the **Key Point** for the lesson. For example, this week's prayer might be: "Lord God, today we celebrate with great joy that a Savior has been born to us. He is the long-expected Messiah, the Christ, and Your only-begotten Son, our Lord. Grant that we may place all our faith in Him alone. In Jesus' name we pray. Amen." After the prayer, sing or say the hymn(s) together. Then read the Bible lesson, review introductory material, and begin the opening questions.

1. Christmas is a particularly appropriate day to celebrate the Lord's Supper because the flesh and blood that Christ took from the Virgin Mary in the incarnation is today given for us to eat and drink for the forgiveness of our sins. In His body and blood, we receive all the benefits of His saving work and have Communion with Him. It is a wonderful and comforting privilege for us to be so closely united with our Lord, who remains bone of our bone and flesh of our flesh for eternity.

2. The angel said to the shepherds, "I bring *you* good news of a great joy that will be for *all the people*. For unto *you* is born this day in the city of David a Savior, who is Christ the Lord" (Luke 2:10–11). *You* are the reason for the season. The celebration of the Lord's birth is all about what God has done for you through His Son. Jesus has no need of a season for Himself. He did not become incarnate for His own sake. As God, He has always existed (John 1:1–2). He is the Creator of all things (John 1:3). He does not just have life; He *is* life (John 1:4). If someone says to you, "Jesus is the reason for the season" this year, remind them that Christmas is also about them—that God loved them enough to come join us in our messy world to save us.

3. Believers in Christ are frequently called children of God (e.g., John 1:12). Those who confess the name of Jesus and are born of water and the Spirit (John 3:5) are given the right to become children of God. Since we are in Christ, who is the Son of God, we also are children of God. Just as Christ prayed and the Father heard His prayers, so, too, are we children free to pray, "Our Father, who art in heaven . . . ." We can be certain that He hears us. Yet, like children who are disappointed that they did not get the toy they wanted,

we often are unsatisfied with the Father's gifts to us. The humble gifts that God gives in Word and Sacrament do not seem as exciting as the festivities of the season. God patiently forgives our ingratitude and keeps seeking us out to call us to repentance, just as good parents do for their children.

4. "Grandpa, tell me a story!" When we read our children bedtime stories, most of them are made-up. It seems that the word *story* most often brings to mind fictional accounts. (A sixth-grade member at a Lutheran church told her VBS teacher that Genesis 2 was a "made-up story about Adam and Eve—they weren't real people.") We must be careful about our use of the word *story* when we are referring to the factual accounts of the Bible. Perhaps we should call them "true stories" or "narratives" or "accounts" or "events." After all, our salvation depends on the truth of the stories of Jesus' saving acts in history.

God Speaks

1. Luke tells us that he wants to set down an orderly account for Theophilus so that he could have certainty concerning the things he had been taught (Luke 1:3–4). Luke's goal was to write an accurate narrative that would build up Theophilus' faith. This shows us that he was very concerned about keeping his facts straight. In Luke 2:1–2, we find out that Caesar Augustus, leader of the Roman Empire, required his subjects to register. This registration was basically a census, and there is historical evidence of a number of these occurring in that period of time. Joseph and Mary, just like everyone else in the Roman Empire, had to be counted in the census. Luke mentions Caesar Augustus in order to locate Jesus' birth as a significant event in world history. Although most people would overlook this event as insignificant, Luke's readers would have seen the cosmic significance of Christ's birth. His message is just as relevant to our gigantic world today.

2. Jesus, as the Christ, would succeed His ancestor David on the throne of Israel. Micah prophesied that even though Bethlehem was insignificant, the Messiah would come from there (Micah 5:2). This Messiah, like His ancestor David, would be a shepherd. Indeed, He would be the Good Shepherd who would secure salvation for His flock. That is why it is so fitting that the first people to have heard the news of Jesus' birth were the shepherds watching their flocks by night. These men realized the importance of a watchful shepherd who is willing to put his own life at risk for the flock.

3. Many people thought that the Messiah would be a power and glory ruler who would restore the kingdom of Israel to its former glory. As He was being

crucified, some people taunted Him because they thought only a show of power would prove that He was the Messiah (Luke 23:35, 39). Peter's great confession of Jesus as the Christ in Matthew 16 is immediately followed by his denial that the Christ could ever suffer and die. He, too, expected a powerful Messiah. Even after the Resurrection, Jesus' followers did not understand what kind of Messiah He was. They asked Him, "Lord, will You at this time restore the kingdom to Israel?" (Acts 1:6). If they had studied Isaiah 52:13–53:12 carefully, they would have been looking for a Messiah who would suffer and die for the sins of the people.

4. John 3:16 is a remarkable encapsulation of the Gospel. It is true that God loves the world so much, but when John writes that "God so loved the world," he means that "God loved the world in this way." Then he goes on to explain the way that God loved the world: by giving His only Son. That giving does not just refer to the incarnation but also to His Son's suffering and death. He gave His all for us.

We Live

1. Humility is perhaps the chief Christian virtue. God looks on the humble estate of His servants and exalts them (Luke 1:48, 52). This does not necessarily mean that the humble will be exalted in this life. But He does desire humility in His followers. As the parable of the wedding feast (Luke 14:7–11) shows, we ought not think too highly of ourselves. This is made most apparent by God's Law, which points out how utterly sinful we are. Each Christian should recognize himself or herself as the chief of sinners who has no merit or worthiness before God. Humility is a gift from God. It goes along with faith. We are humbled before God, and when we are freed by the Gospel, we recognize that we can humbly serve each other without worrying about social status or pride.

2. Jesus loved (and loves) infants and all children. He laid His hands on them and blessed them. This certainly reminds us of His gracious work in baptizing infants, thus bringing them into His Kingdom. As infants and little children are completely dependent on their parents, so are we dependent on our Lord for everything. Adults must daily learn to be children before the Lord, as Jesus says: "Whoever does not receive the kingdom of God like a child shall not enter it" (Luke 18:17).

3. People realize that they need saving from all sorts of things. They look to doctors to save them from poor health and death. They look to entertainers to save them from boredom. They look to good jobs and the stock market to save

them from financial problems. These temporal saviors all have their function in society, but Jesus came to "save His people from their sins" (Matthew 1:21). John the Baptist would go before Jesus "to give knowledge of salvation to His people in the forgiveness of their sins" (Luke 1:77). When we say that Jesus saves us from our sins, we need to be careful to remember that this means the forgiveness for sins. It does not mean that Jesus will take away all of the sins of Christians to the extent that they do not sin anymore. We remain both sinner and saint. But Jesus saves us from the *guilt* of our sins, for which we deserve damnation. Our dying world that seeks salvation in so many places needs a Savior, one who will forgive the people's sins and make them right again with God.

4. We are more blessed than the shepherds because we know the whole story, while they only saw part of it. The realities of the Church share the full story and salvation of our Lord. When the Gospel is preached and we hear it in faith, it saves us from our sins. When we are baptized, we are united with Christ's death and resurrection. When we eat Christ's body and blood, we are as close to Him as even Mary ever was. While it is fun to imagine what that night was like, the Word and Sacraments are not imaginary signs of grace— they actually deliver salvation to us. How blessed are we!

Closing

Encourage the adults with children in Sunday School to review their child's Growing in Christ Leaflet together at home.

For the **Family Connections** section, encourage the class to study the Small Catechism at home regularly, especially if they have children. Children are able to memorize well, and the catechism will be a great asset for them throughout their lives. If students in the class do not have catechisms for themselves and their children, see if the church has copies available for distribution.

Lesson 5

The Boy Jesus in the Temple
Luke 2:41–52

Opening

Open class with a prayer tied to the **Key Point** for the lesson. For example, this week's prayer could be: "Lord God, Your Son, Jesus, loved to dwell in Your house. Instill in us a fervent desire to come often to Your house to hear Your Word, hear that Jesus is our Savior, and receive Your gifts of forgiveness and salvation for His sake. In Jesus' name. Amen." After the prayer, sing or say the hymn(s) together. Then read the Bible lesson, review introductory material, and begin the opening questions.

1. John 20:30–31 says that the purpose of John's Gospel—and this could apply to the whole Bible—is "so that you may believe that Jesus is the Christ, the Son of God, and that by believing you may have life in His name." John 21:25 says that the world is not big enough to contain all of the books that could be written about Him. Clearly, the Holy Spirit decided that the events of Jesus' childhood and adolescence need not be our concern. The stories would most certainly be delightful, but they may have only distracted us from the things we really need to know about Jesus for salvation, which are abundantly revealed in Scripture.

2. Luke emphasizes in his introduction that he consulted with people who were eyewitnesses of the things that took place in his Gospel. Though we can never know for certain, the great detail Luke provides about Jesus' conception, infancy, and childhood could very well have come from Mary's own recollections. That would not have been the first time the Holy Spirit used Mary to bring about His purposes.

3. Jerusalem was the city of peace and was where God dwelled in His temple. It was the center of worship for all faithful children of Israel. Luke highlights Jesus' presence in Jerusalem as a child in order to emphasize that God had become incarnate and would now dwell among His people in the flesh. Jesus announces in Luke 18 that He would go to Jerusalem to fulfill the Father's will as the One who would suffer, die, and rise again to save His people. Luke 24 points out that Jerusalem would be the initial location of the apostles' mission, once they receive the Holy Spirit, the power from on high, at

Pentecost. Christians are members of the New Jerusalem, the Christian Church, and look forward to an eternal Jerusalem in heaven.

God Speaks

1. The fact that Jesus went to the Passover as a child hints at His role as "the Lamb of God who takes away the sin of the world" (John 1:29). Luke makes it a point to tell us that on "the day of Unleavened Bread," the "Passover lamb had to be sacrificed" (Luke 22:7). Though Jesus would not be crucified until the next day, Luke's language suggests that Jesus was the true Passover lamb. As the body of a sacrificed lamb is given for an offering and then eaten, and as the blood of the lamb is spilled, now Jesus gives His true body and blood to eat and drink under the bread and wine for the forgiveness of sins. The Passover Feast had now been fulfilled and replaced by a greater one—the Lord's Supper.

2. In Luke 2:49, Jesus says that He needs to be in His Father's house, even while Joseph is standing right there. It is clear that God is His Father. In Luke 1:35, Jesus is called the "Son of God." In 10:22, Jesus speaks of His relationship as the Son to the Father. In 22:29 and 24:49, He also speaks of God as His Father. The Scriptures are clear that Jesus is not less God than the Father. In John 10:30, Jesus says, "I and the Father are one." In the Nicene Creed, we confess that Jesus is "begotten, not made; being of one substance with the Father, by whom all things were made." It is a great mystery of our faith but true nonetheless. Jesus is true God and true man at the same time.

3. Jesus' humanity is apparent throughout this lesson. In Luke 2:42, we see that He was twelve years old, reminding us of His earthly birth. In 2:46, we see Him asking questions and learning from the teachers. In 2:51, we hear that He was submissive to His parents. And in 2:52, we learn that Jesus "increased in wisdom and in stature." We call Jesus' time on earth before His resurrection from the dead (technically before His revivification and descent into hell) His state of humiliation. During this time, Jesus usually chose not to use His powers and privileges as God. Philippians 2 and Hebrews 5 speak of this state. He humbled Himself and became obedient even to the cross to save us. It is a great mystery how Jesus could both know all things and yet learn. We must simply bow in reverence to this awesome truth that God and man are one in Jesus.

4. We cannot be entirely certain why Mary and Joseph did not understand Jesus' words and actions. Perhaps God chose to hide the knowledge from

them for a time. Perhaps the twelve years that had passed since Jesus' birth had been unremarkable, and they thought that He was just a normal kid. In Mark 3:20–21, we see that Jesus' family thought that He had lost His mind because so many people were following Him. Those closest to Jesus often completely misunderstood Him. In Luke 9:44–45 and 18:31–34, Jesus' disciples had the truth about Jesus' upcoming death concealed from them, which could only be done by God. Why some people believe and others do not will always be a mystery to us.

5. Luke 4:43 indicates that Jesus was compelled to preach the Gospel. Preaching was part of His divinely ordained mission. Luke 9:22 says that Jesus had to suffer many things, be rejected by the leaders of Jerusalem, be killed, and rise again. Luke 17:25 says that Jesus had to be rejected by the entire generation. On the cross, He was completely alone, forsaken by even God. The Gospels are appropriately labeled "Passion narratives with long introductions." God chose to give His own Son into death to save us. It was necessary; it had to happen.

We Live

1. The purpose of confirmation is to guide Christians into a deeper under-standing and appreciation of the faith that was given to them in Baptism. Students learn Luther's Small Catechism, which is a wonderful guide to Christian doctrine, faith, and life. They study the Bible and memorize key verses. They are taught the great blessings of the Sacrament of the Altar and what proper self-examination is. In the confirmation rite, they have an oppor-tunity to make a public confession of their faith.

Confirmation is not absolutely necessary. It is not a sacrament. It also is not necessarily a prerequisite to admission to the Lord's Supper. Confirmation is not an end in itself. It is not graduation from church as some have described it. Rather, it is a means to help people understand their dependence on the Lord's mercy, which is shown to them weekly in the Divine Service. We pray that confirmands (like Jesus in the temple) acquire an appreciation of the riches of Scripture that can be mined through a lifetime of Bible classes and devotions. And hopefully they will be motivated to bring their own children into the Lord's arms in Baptism and to His house every Sunday.

We can encourage our own children when they are in confirmation by taking an interest in what they are learning and by having a positive attitude toward the inconveniences associated with travel to and from church frequently. We can encourage adults who are going through catechesis by attending classes with them and offering to answer questions that they might be embarrassed to ask of the pastor.

2. Jesus tells us about His saving work when He says that He "came not to be served but to serve, and to give His life as a ransom for many" (Matthew 20:28). At the same time, He provides the perfect example of Christian love and service through His actions. The disciples of Jesus are not to think of themselves but are to be servants to each other.

3. As Jesus stands trial before the Sanhedrin, He is accused of claiming to destroy the Jerusalem temple and build another one without human hands (Mark 14:58). As He suffered on the cross, He was mocked by those who said that if He was strong enough to destroy and rebuild the temple in three days, He should be able to come down from the cross (Mark 15:29–30). Yet these people did not realize that Jesus would rebuild the temple precisely by dying and rising again. In John 2:18–22, Jesus locates the new temple in His own flesh. He indicates that the presence of God will now be located wherever He is. The temple of His body would be destroyed, but on the third day He would rise triumphant over Satan and all His enemies. We no longer need to go to a temple made of human hands (Acts 7:48), but we find the true temple in Jesus. The new dwelling place of God in the world is in Christ's body, the Church. The presence of God is found in the flesh and blood of Jesus to which we are joined in Baptism and with which we are fed in the Lord's Supper.

Closing

Encourage the adults with children in Sunday School to review their child's Growing in Christ Leaflet together at home.

For the **Family Connections** section, encourage the class to study the Small Catechism at home regularly, especially if they have children. Children are able to memorize well, and the catechism will be a great asset for them throughout their lives. If students in the class do not have catechisms for themselves and their children, see if the church has copies available for distribution.

Lesson 6

The Baptism of Jesus

Luke 3:15–22

Opening

Open class with a prayer tied to the **Key Point** for the lesson. For example, this week's prayer could be: "Heavenly Father, You sent the Holy Spirit at Jesus' Baptism to announce that He is Your beloved Son. In Baptism, You have made us Your children through the work of the Holy Spirit. Remind us of this wonderful gift often and help us to be thankful for it. In Jesus' name. Amen." After the prayer, sing or say the hymn(s) together. Then read the Bible lesson, review introductory material, and begin the opening questions.

1. The Father speaks from heaven, "You are My beloved Son; with You I am well pleased" (Luke 3:22). The Holy Spirit descended on Jesus in bodily form like a dove. Here we have Jesus revealed as true God and true man. Here we have God revealed as Father, Son, and Holy Spirit—three persons, one God. The mysteries of the incarnation and Trinity are spoken of here. The God of our salvation reveals Himself to us in human flesh. These revelations are what Epiphany is all about.

2. Baptism is valid whether it is done with water from any kind of font—or water from anywhere, for that matter—since the connection of God's Word with water makes the Baptism what it is. However, a congregation might choose to have an ornate font or display it prominently in order to confess visually that Baptism is an important part of the Church's faith and life. Also, when worshipers see the font, they will be reminded of their own Baptism.

God Speaks

1. John was a sinner just like us, and he knew it. He was a servant of the Lord, not the Christ. He did not want followers of his own but wanted to prepare the way for Jesus and point to Him, saying, "Behold, the Lamb of God, who takes away the sin of the world" (John 1:29). John said, "He must increase, but I must decrease" (John 3:30). He is a model for each pastor, who is not in the Office of the Holy Ministry for his own sake but for the sake of magnifying Christ. A true pastor will always point away from himself and toward Jesus.

2. John's Baptism had several differences from Christian Baptism, but Luke 3:3 does say that his Baptism was "for the forgiveness of sins." When Jesus

went to the Jordan River to be baptized by John, it wasn't because He needed the forgiveness that was offered in Baptism. And John knew this. That's why Matthew 3:14 has John the Baptist recorded as saying in effect, "I need to be baptized by you, Jesus. You don't need to be baptized by me. I'm the sinner . . . you're the savior!" But Jesus knew better. Matthew 3:15 has Jesus saying in effect, "I know what I'm doing, John. Baptize me, so we can fulfill all righteousness." Jesus was undergoing a Baptism for sinners so that He could become the world's biggest sinner. When He was baptized, He took upon himself the sins of the whole world. By receiving Baptism, Jesus was now basically saying, "I now stand in the place of all the sinners in the world. The weight of the world's sins rests upon My shoulders. And I am on a mission to make atonement for all sins. I am going to carry them to the cross and die, destroying these sins with Me." In Baptism, our sins become His, and His righteousness becomes ours (2 Corinthians 5:21).

3. Isaiah 42:1 says that the Holy Spirit will be put upon the Father's Servant, who is Jesus. With the opened heaven and the Spirit's descent in bodily form, the Spirit's presence gives testimony as do the Father's words: "You are My beloved Son; with you I am well pleased" (Luke 3:22). Here, the Holy Trinity is present to mark the beginning of Jesus' work of salvation as the Messiah. The Son will baptize people with the Holy Spirit (Luke 3:16), and the Spirit will give entrance to the kingdom of God (John 3:5). The Holy Spirit makes people holy.

4. The fact that Jesus underwent Baptism helps us understand why He sent His apostles out to make disciples by baptizing and teaching (Matthew 28:19–20). Jesus' life is paradigmatic for them, for they, too, would call on people to repent and be baptized for the forgiveness of their sins (Acts 2:38).

We Live

1. John the Baptist proclaims that Jesus will burn up the chaff—those who do not believe in Him—with unquenchable fire. Jesus speaks words of grace and wrath. Those who believe in Him will have everlasting life, but those who reject Him will receive eternal punishment. This passage graphically reminds us that Jesus, on the Last Day, will render a judgment on all of humankind, and not everyone will receive a verdict of not guilty. Today, people think that Jesus is tame—He's everybody's friend and would never judge anyone. But we must never lose the proclamation of both Law and Gospel in the Church, for without the preaching of God's wrath, people will never appreciate the

wonderful message that Christ has earned forgiveness for us and we no longer have to fear condemnation.

2. "Our Father who art in heaven" can only be prayed by children of the heavenly Father. Our Baptism follows the pattern of the Son's Baptism. When someone is baptized, the Father says from above, "You are My beloved son (or daughter); with you I am well pleased" (Luke 3:22). Paul tells us that, since we are "in Christ Jesus," we are all "sons of God, through faith," because those who "were baptized into Christ have put on Christ" (Galatians 3:26–27).

When we pray, "Hallowed be Thy name," we confess the holiness of God's name, "Father, Son, and Holy Spirit" (Matthew 28:19–20). That is the name that is put upon us at Baptism. We are made holy by God's holy name. Jesus has revealed the Father to us. Believing in Jesus' name, we believe in the name of God and He has given us the right to be called "children of God" (John 1:12–13).

The prayer, "Thy kingdom come," means that we ask for God's kingdom to come to us, for our salvation. "Unless one is born of water and the Spirit, he cannot enter the kingdom of God" (John 3:5). The kingdom of God has come to us in Baptism, and we pray that His future kingdom would come when we finally will see Him face-to-face.

When we pray, "Forgive us our trespasses," we are confessing that we frequently sin and continually need forgiveness. Yet forgiveness does not come to us without means. That is why the Lord gives it out so abundantly through Word and Sacrament. Baptism gives the forgiveness of sins (Acts 2:38), not just once but daily and richly.

Closing

Encourage the adults with children in Sunday School to review their child's Growing in Christ Leaflet together at home.

In the **Personal Reflection** section, Luther's Flood Prayer suggests that any water we come across—in the shower, when it's raining, and so on—can and should remind us of our Baptism.

Lesson 7
Jesus Changes Water into Wine
John 2:1–11

Opening

Open class with a prayer tied to the **Key Point** for the lesson. For example, this week's prayer could be: "Heavenly Father, through His first miracle, Jesus revealed Himself to be one with You, Your one and only Son. Continue to reveal Yourself to us through the earthly means of Word, water, bread, and wine, imparting the forgiveness Christ earned for us. In His name we pray. Amen." After the prayer, sing or say the hymn(s) together. Then read the Bible lesson, review introductory material, and begin the opening questions.

1. Like anyone, Jesus experienced the ups and downs of life. There were times of feasting, fasting, and famine. So it is with us. God blesses us with wonderful and happy times, when it is right to feast on the gifts He gives. Other times, we must focus on fasting and prayer. And He also sends us times of famine when we struggle and mourn. In all these things, our lives are being conformed to the pattern of Christ. We neither "feast sumptuously every day" like the rich man (Luke 16:19), nor fast all the time like a works-righteous monk, nor suffer pain and deprivation continually, but we experience the full range of human experience as Jesus did.

2. Jesus upholds creation with His almighty power and protects us from all harm and danger. We can take great comfort that the One who has redeemed us with His own blood also uses His power for our help and protection.

3. As sinners, we tend not to always freely give our best to others but often do just enough to make ourselves look good and no more. We are concerned with our own image; not so with God. He gives freely of all that He is, and has saved the best for last—our resurrection on the Last Day.

God Speaks

1. This is the first narrative of Jesus' activity in John's Gospel, so clearly it is of fundamental importance. It functioned to reveal who Jesus is to the disciples with the result that they believed in Him (or that their faith in Him was strengthened). All of John's signs reveal things about the person of Jesus and describe the resulting belief of His followers. The point of all of John's

stories is to focus on Jesus as the one sent by the Father to bring salvation to the world. What shines through in the signs is His glory, fulfilling the promise made to Nathanael in John 1:50, "You will see greater things than these." John explicitly describes the purpose of the signs—and the purpose of his entire Gospel—when he says, "Now Jesus did many other signs in the presence of the disciples, which are not written in this book; but these are written so that you may believe that Jesus is the Christ, the Son of God, and that by believing you may have life in His name" (John 20:30–31).

2. This miracle demonstrates that the Messianic age is at hand, because of the amazing quality and abundance of the wine Jesus makes. The Jews expected that one characteristic of the Messianic age would be a great abundance of fine wine. According to Psalm 104:15, wine is a sign of joy and gladness from the Lord. Isaiah 25:6 says that the Lord will make for all peoples (Jews and Gentiles): "A feast of rich food, a feast of well-aged wine." Amos 9:13 says that "the mountains shall drip sweet wine, and all the hills shall flow with it." Jesus' miracle is a sign that these prophecies have been fulfilled in His very person. In Mark 2:22, Jesus indicates that His presence in the world has brought about a new era, a new testament, that is too great to fit into any of the old covenants God previously made with Israel. This New Testament will also include the Gentiles. Jesus is the new wine for the Church, which is a fresh wineskin. The old wineskins, like the Jewish purification rites, have passed away. The water of Jewish purification rites has given way to the choicest wines that Jesus brings. Jesus is the only way to the Father. All previous religious structures, customs, and feasts lose meaning in His presence because He has fulfilled them. This miracle dramatically shows the movement from the lesser to the greater.

3. In the Old Testament, God is often described as the bridegroom of His people, His bride. At weddings in Jesus' day, it was the ultimate responsibility of the bridegroom to provide wine for the feast. Though Jesus is not the bridegroom at this wedding, He fulfills the bridegroom's function by providing an abundance of wine. That is why it is so fitting for Jesus to manifest His glory at a wedding. John the Baptist says in John 3:29 that he is, in a manner of speaking, only the best man, not the bridegroom. The bridegroom is Christ, who has the bride, the Church, as Paul describes in Ephesians 5:25–27.

4. In John 7:30, it becomes clear that Jesus' hour will involve being arrested. In 12:23–24, Jesus indicates that His hour of glorification would be on the

cross, when the grain of wheat falls into the ground and dies. In 13:1, we learn that His hour would involve Him departing this world and loving His own until the end. In 17:1, right before His Passion, He prays to the Father because His hour had come. When Jesus responds to His mother that His hour has not yet come, He is introducing the important theme of the hour of His crucifixion, which all of His signs point toward. Even though He will give a glimpse of His glory in the miracle at Cana, He will not give a full revelation of Himself until the cross.

5. John 1:14 shows that Jesus' glory is that He is "the only Son from the Father, full of grace and truth," who has become flesh and dwells among us. In John 2:11, He manifested His glory as the Son of God through the miracle at Cana. In 8:54, the fact that He is God's Son is reiterated, showing the source of His glory. John 12:23–24 says that the hour of Jesus' glorification is at hand, and He speaks of His crucifixion when He describes a grain of wheat that falls into the earth and dies. In 17:1, right before Jesus' Passion, Jesus prays to His Father, "the hour has come; glorify Your Son that the Son may glorify You." The linking of the words *glory* and *hour* reminds us that Jesus' glory will be in His sacrificial death for sinners. In John 19:2–3, Jesus is portrayed as a king as He receives a crown of thorns, a purple robe, and mocking praise from the soldiers. In 19:19, Jesus is given the title "King of the Jews." As kings are normally given much glory, the great surprise of John's Gospel (and of *the* Gospel) is that the Son of God's true glory is revealed in a shameful crucifixion. He had revealed the glory He possessed as God through various signs, but then turned everything upside down by showing that the hour of glory He had continually moved toward was the hour of the cross.

We Live

1. Signs reveal who Jesus is, but that does not mean people will receive them and believe in who He is. God reveals Himself in His Word but He does not compel people to believe it; He lets Himself be rejected. Throughout Jesus' ministry, He encountered many who witnessed His miracles but did not grasp the underlying sign. After He fed the five thousand, the crowd and disciples came looking for Him. "Jesus answered them, 'Truly, truly, I say to you, you are seeking Me, not because you saw signs, but because you ate your fill of the loaves'" (John 6:26). They wanted to make Him a bread king, one who would always keep them well-fed (John 6:34). But in that case, the real point of Jesus' miracle was to reveal that He is the bread of life (John 6:35). Those who were concerned only for their bellies did not believe in Him. Thus,

making visible or revealing does not always end in belief. Today, many people still want Jesus to perform miracles for them, such as healing their diseases or turning around their finances. While He *could* do these things, He has revealed in the Gospel that He wants to save people from their sins and be the bread of life, not simply bread that spoils.

2. The purification jars were used for various rites of washing before meals and other activities. In John 3:5, Jesus says that only those born of water and the Spirit will enter the kingdom of God. The transition from the old purification jars and rites to the new wine of Jesus is suggestive of Christian Baptism, of Jesus cleansing people of their sins. Paul tells us in Ephesians 5:25–27 that Christ has sanctified the Church through the washing of water with the Word, so that she will be holy and without blemish.

3. The blood and water that pour out of Jesus' side in John 19:34 have long been interpreted as an important connection between the Sacraments and Jesus' death. The Sacraments get their saving power through Jesus' death and resurrection. 1 John 5:6–8 is often interpreted as a reference to the cross, where Jesus gave up His Spirit and the blood and water flowed from His side: "This is He who came by water and blood—Jesus Christ; not by the water only but by the water and the blood. And the Spirit is the one who testifies, because the Spirit is the truth. For there are three that testify: the Spirit and the water and the blood; and these three agree." 1 John 1:7 says that "The blood of Jesus His Son cleanses us from all sin." In Holy Baptism, we are washed in the blood of Jesus and made spotless. In the Lord's Supper, we drink Jesus' true blood to receive the forgiveness of our sins. Both of these Sacraments are gifts directly from Christ's bloody sacrifice for our sins on the cross.

Closing

Encourage the adults with children in Sunday School to review their child's Growing in Christ Leaflet together at home.

For the **Family Connections** section, encourage the class to study the Small Catechism at home regularly, especially if they have children.

Lesson 8

Jesus Rejected at Nazareth
Luke 4:16–30

Opening

Open class with a prayer tied to the **Key Point** for the lesson. For example, this week's prayer could be: "Lord God, You do not force people to believe in You, but let Yourself be rejected. Yet You have clearly shown us that Jesus is Your only Son and have given us the gift of faith. Preserve our faith in Jesus. In His name we pray. Amen." After the prayer, sing or say the hymn(s) together. Then read the Bible lesson, review introductory material, and begin the opening questions.

1. Teaching was done almost exclusively orally in Jesus' day. Only the Old Testament was written, but those documents were on bulky scrolls. What we think of as a book only began to arise in the third century AD with the usage of parchment instead of papyrus. Until the printing press was invented in the fifteenth century, books were copied by hand and extremely expensive. It was much later still that books could be printed inexpensively. Even if the people had had personal copies of the Hebrew Scriptures, it is unlikely that they would have been trained to read them, since Hebrew had given way to Aramaic and Greek in popular speech and writing. Oral proclamation was the primary vehicle for teaching, but there was more to Jesus' preaching than the imparting of head knowledge. His Word had—and has—the power to create faith, since His words are "spirit and life" (John 6:63).

2. Often the word *amen* is translated "truly" in the Bible. Martin Luther explained in his explanation to the Conclusion of the Lord's Prayer in the Small Catechism that *Amen* means "Yes, it shall be so." He explains that, in relation to the Lord's Prayer, *Amen* "means that I should be certain that these petitions are pleasing to our Father in heaven, and are heard by Him; for He Himself has commanded us to pray in this way and has promised to hear us." It is an expression of confidence in what we confess or pray.

3. Most of us have encountered the cheek-pinching older person who is fond of reminding you, "I remember when you were knee-high to a grasshopper." We often make judgments on people's abilities and personalities based on what we know of their past. To the people of Nazareth, Jesus seemed ordinary; He was just Joseph's son. Perhaps this can partially explain why the

people of Nazareth were slow to believe in Him. Yet on a more profound level, the reason the people of Nazareth rejected Jesus was that He was a true prophet, and all of God's prophets faced rejection at the hands of the people of their native place.

God Speaks

1a. Jesus describes His teaching ministry in terms that will recur throughout Luke's Gospel. He will proclaim "good news to the poor," "liberty to the captives," and "the year of the Lord's favor." He will perform miracles that will give recovery of sight to the blind and "set at liberty those who are oppressed" (4:18–19). In 4:31–37, Jesus demonstrates His role as teacher and miracle worker. The people in Capernaum were astonished at the authority with which He taught, and they were amazed at His control over demons. Luke 4:38–41 also describe Jesus' healing ministry, and 4:42–44 describe His preaching.

1b. Since we know the whole story of Jesus' life, it is easy to see that His rejection and attempted murder at the hands of the people of Nazareth point forward to His ultimate rejection and death on a cross. It was not yet His time to die for the sins of the people, so He miraculously escapes their grip. In Luke 13:31–34, Jesus says that He will continue His teaching and healing ministries until the day He fulfills His role as a true prophet by dying in Jerusalem. We again are reminded that no prophet is welcome in his hometown, since the Old Testament prophets in Jerusalem were often threatened with death. Yet Jesus shows His love for all people because He continues to press on toward Jerusalem to die for His enemies.

2. Sin is an oppressive force in our lives. It destroys relationships and causes all kinds of maladies. We are all like sheep who constantly go after our own sinful way of doing things. Sin will be a reality for us until we die. In that sense, we are still oppressed by sin. Yet Jesus' perfect obedience and atoning death won forgiveness for the iniquity, or guilt, of our sin. Though the oppressive effects of sin are still evident in our lives, God no longer holds us guilty for the sins we commit, since Jesus would "give knowledge of salvation to his people in the forgiveness of their sins" (Luke 1:77). Through the preaching of the Gospel and giving out of the Sacraments, our sins are forgiven through faith, since Jesus arranged that "repentance and forgiveness of sins should be proclaimed in His name to all nations" (Luke 24:47).

3. As Jesus proclaims Isaiah 61, He identifies the Holy Trinity. He says that "the [Holy] Spirit of the Lord [Father] is upon Me [the Son]." This statement points back to His Baptism by John in the Jordan, where we hear that "the Holy Spirit descended on him in bodily form, like a dove; and a voice came from heaven, 'You are My beloved Son; with You I am well pleased'" (Luke 3:22). At that time, the Trinity also was revealed. We also are told that Jesus is the "Anointed One," the Christ or Messiah, in Acts 10:38, "God [the Father] anointed Jesus of Nazareth [the Son] with the Holy Spirit and with power." We see that knowledge of the Holy Trinity is not unimportant but is essential to understanding who God is and how He has revealed Himself to us in Jesus.

4. Jesus Christ is said to have created all things "in heaven and on earth, visible and invisible" (Colossians 1:16). He is true God and true man, and has made peace between God and Man through His blood. He has reconciled all things to Himself, everything in the creation (Colossians 1:20). This teaching is found in Luke 4:18–19, since Jesus is said to bring justice where there is injustice, healing where there is sickness, and forgiveness where there is the oppression of sin.

5. The Old Testament Church had the Year of Jubilee every fifty years. Every debt was forgiven, every Jewish slave was set free, and every piece of property went back to its original owner. That physical Year of Jubilee foreshadowed the real one Jesus announced in Nazareth. The Lord came to freely cancel all debts of sin. Thanks to Jesus, sinners are liberated from sin, death, and the power of the devil. In Jesus, we find a constant year of the Lord's favor.

We Live

1. Jesus referred to the prophecy from Isaiah 61 that the Messiah would come and proclaim the Gospel to a fallen creation. He indicates that He was the reason that Isaiah 61 was written. He brought Isaiah's prophecy into reality through His preaching. His Word is powerful. It does what it says. As Creator, He spoke the world into existence. Now He speaks, and the sick are healed and sinners are forgiven. Today, Jesus continues to preach to His Church through pastors in order to forgive sinners and save the lost. As Paul says, "It pleased God through the folly of what we preach to save those who believe" (1 Corinthians 1:21). What is that preaching about? "We preach Christ crucified," Paul says (1 Corinthians 1:23).

2. The synagogue was where Jewish believers assembled to hear the Old Testament read and explained. This was the perfect location for the apostles to proclaim that Jesus was the Jewish Messiah. In Acts 9:20, right after Paul's conversion, he begins to preach in the synagogues that Jesus is the Son of God. In 13:5, we learn that Paul and Barnabas proclaimed the Word of God in the synagogues. In 14:1, we find that they brought a great number of Jews and Greeks to faith through their preaching in the synagogue. The synagogue provided great opportunities for the expansion of the Church. Today, the message at church is still the same—Jesus is the Son of God, the Messiah, the Word of God is proclaimed—and people are still brought to faith through that preaching. That is why our goal in evangelism is always to bring people to church, where the Word of God does its work.

3. When we ask the question "Why?" to God, we are setting ourselves up for disappointment. "Why?" is not a question we are entitled to ask Him. Of course, God could eradicate all death and disease in an instant. He can grant miracles whenever He wants. But what He really desires from us is faith in His Gospel. As Hebrews 11:1 says, "Faith is the assurance of things hoped for, the conviction of things not seen." Because of our sinful weakness, we want God to show His power with miracles and signs. But what He has given us is His Word of promise, which tells of Jesus' resurrection and our future resurrection, when there will be no more tears. The greatest miracle God has performed for us is giving us the gift of faith, through His Word and Sacraments.

Closing

Encourage the adults with children in Sunday School to review their child's Growing in Christ Leaflet together at home.

Lesson 9

Jesus Heals Many
Luke 4:31–44

Opening

Open class with a prayer tied to the **Key Point** for the lesson. For example, this week's prayer could be: "Lord God, through many miracles, Your Son Jesus showed us His power over sin and the devil. Help us to trust in the forgiveness of sins He gives us and rejoice in His triumph over the devil. In Jesus' name we pray. Amen." After the prayer, sing or say the hymn(s) together. Then read the Bible lesson, review introductory material, and read together the opening section.

God Speaks

1. An unclean demon would be tormented by being close to the holy One of God. Demons, being servants of the devil, hate God. They cry out when they come into the presence of God in Christ. James 2:19 says that even the demons believe in God (so much for atheists), and they shudder! They recognize that their days are numbered because of God's victory over them in Christ. When Jesus comes preaching the Gospel that sins are freely forgiven for His sake, this exposes the demon. As long as the demon felt no threat, he was silent. But now, the demon must try to denounce Jesus and keep everyone in the synagogue from seeing who Jesus truly is. Though they are silenced by Jesus, the demons do confirm to the reader of the Gospel that Jesus is the Messiah, the "Holy One of God" (4:34), as well as the "Son of God" (4:41). Only later do the disciples come to understand these things about Jesus.

2. Luke 9:18–20 provides the first instance in Luke's Gospel of a confession that Jesus is the Christ given by a person who witnessed Jesus' ministry. Peter, speaking on behalf of the other disciples, calls Jesus "the Christ of God." Yet in 9:21, Jesus gives strict orders not to tell anyone, just as He had previously instructed the demons not to tell anyone that He was the Christ. Jesus predicts His rejection by the Jewish leaders, Passion, and resurrection. But it seems that He was not yet ready for this to occur—He still had many things to accomplish. That is why He told them not to reveal who He was. As John 11:47–48 shows, the Jewish leaders saw Jesus as a threat that needed to be eliminated. In Matthew 2:1–4, the wicked King Herod wanted to destroy the King of the Jews who had been born in his territory, so Jesus' family had

to flee into Egypt for safety. In today's lesson, Jesus' hour was not yet at hand, so He withheld His full identity until later.

3. The seventy-two healed the sick and proclaimed that "The kingdom of God has come near to you" (Luke 10:9). Jesus sent these men out as His messengers to reveal that the kingdom of God had come. They preached the Gospel of forgiveness. Their miracles showed that the King had authority over the creation and was restoring it. Anyone who rejects the kingdom of God will face a worse fate than the ancient city of Sodom, which perished under fire and brimstone. In Luke 18:16, Jesus says that the kingdom of God belongs to infants. We receive King Jesus in simple faith, just as little children trust in their parents for everything. We are freely given admittance into the kingdom of God through Baptism (John 3:5).

4. Jesus first gives the paralytic what he really needs—forgiveness. Then, in order to demonstrate His authority to forgive sins, He heals the man. This offends the scribes and Pharisees, since they recognize that only God can forgive sins. They got it! Jesus was showing Himself to be God, the gracious God who forgives the sins of the ungodly. In John 20, Jesus gives to His apostles, and by extension to the men who would come later in the Office of the Holy Ministry, the authority to forgive sins of the repentant and to withhold forgiveness from the unrepentant.

We Live

1. Some of the people, knowing the Old Testament Scriptures and expecting the Messiah, would have recognized through the miracles that Jesus was the fulfillment of those prophecies. They would have had saving faith in Him, just as they already had saving faith that God would send a Messiah. Yet for the people who only saw Jesus' miracles, they might have concluded that He was just another wonder-worker, as those were very common at the time. Jesus warns the Church, "If anyone says to you, 'Look, here is the Christ!' or 'Look, there he is!' do not believe it. False christs and false prophets will arise and perform signs and wonders" (Mark 13:21–22). For this reason, we must always be very cautious about people who claim to have healing powers and keep our eyes fixed on the Gospel of forgiveness, as Jesus shows us in Luke 5:24. Jesus did miracles in order to demonstrate His authority to forgive sins; modern healers do their work to provide strictly temporal healing or to make money. Yet the healing ministry of Jesus can and should be continued as Christians support programs and institutions that bring healing to people. Many hospitals have been established by church bodies, recalling the great

interest Jesus had in people's health. And these also provide a wonderful opportunity to share what Jesus gives—the forgiveness of sins.

2. First Peter's mother-in-law is healed; then she serves. She is given new life by Jesus. She might have died from her fever. But now that Jesus has saved her from her sickness—without any effort or doing on her part—she does what is given for her to do. She fulfills her vocation as a homemaker. She doesn't go out and become a missionary. She simply continues doing her job. She serves. So also Jesus gives us new life through the forgiveness of sins, and we serve Him by serving our neighbor in our vocations. That serving might include telling others about Jesus, but it is fundamentally to fulfill the duties of our various callings in family, workplace, and Church. Our life is one of service to others. As we pray in the post-Communion collect, we ask that Christ's body and blood "would strengthen us . . . in faith toward [God] and in fervent love toward one another" (*LW*, p. 174).

3. One reason that people reject the Gospel is that they do not believe they need to receive the Lord's forgiveness. They are quite content to hang onto their sins, go it alone, or even deny there are such things as sins. People avoid the Church for the same reasons, or they find churches that do not focus on the forgiveness of sins. But on a deeper level, the reason people reject the Gospel and avoid church is that "The god of this world [Satan] has blinded the minds of the unbelievers, to keep them from seeing the light of the gospel of the glory of Christ, who is the image of God" (2 Corinthians 4:4). And even people who receive the Word of God are at risk: "The devil comes and takes away the word from their hearts, so that they may not believe and be saved" (Luke 8:12). Luther explains that in the Sixth Petition of the Lord's Prayer, "We pray . . . that God would guard and keep us so that the devil, the world, and our sinful nature may not deceive us or mislead us into false belief, despair, and other great shame and vice. Although we are attacked by these things, we pray that we may finally overcome them and win the victory." Satan and his demonic forces are responsible for spreading unbelief throughout the world and in our own hearts. We must constantly be aware of his presence and defend ourselves against him through faithful use of God's Word and Sacraments.

4. Luther often taught that Christ's body and blood helps the whole man, body and soul. Forgiveness of sins is the primary gift, and life and salvation flow from it. We must be careful not to make the Sacrament into a magical cure-all, while at the same time confessing that God can give healing to the whole

person through His Son's body and blood. The bodily nature of the Sacrament also points forward to our future resurrection. We will not spend eternity as disembodied souls but will rise again on the Last Day.

Closing

Encourage the adults with children in Sunday School to review their child's Growing in Christ Leaflet together at home.

If you have time, share these thoughts from the Large Catechism on the Seventh Petition of the Lord's Prayer:

In the Greek text this petition reads, "Deliver or preserve us from the evil one," or "the hateful one." It looks like Jesus was speaking about the devil, like He would summarize every petition in one. So the entire substance of all our prayer is directed against our chief enemy. For it is he who hinders among us everything that we pray for: God's name or honor, God's kingdom and will, our daily bread, a cheerful good conscience, and so forth.

Therefore, we finally sum it all up and say, "Dear Father, grant that we be rid of all these disasters." But there is also included in this petition whatever evil may happen to us under the devil's kingdom: poverty, shame, death, and, in short, all the agonizing misery and heartache of which there is such an unnumbered multitude on the earth. Since the devil is not only a liar, but also a murderer (John 8:44), he constantly seeks our life. He wreaks his vengeance whenever he can afflict our bodies with misfortune and harm. Therefore, it happens that he often breaks men's necks or drives them to insanity, drowns some, and moves many to commit suicide and to many other terrible disasters (e.g., Mark 9:17–22). So there is nothing for us to do upon earth but to pray against this archenemy without stopping. For unless God preserved us, we would not be safe from this enemy even for an hour.

You see again how God wishes for us to pray to Him also for all the things that affect our bodily interests, so that we seek and expect help nowhere else except in Him (LC IV 113–18).

Lesson 10

Jesus Calls the First Disciples
Luke 5:1–11

Opening

Open class with a prayer tied to the **Key Point** for the lesson. For example, this week's prayer could be: "Lord God, Your Son, Jesus, chose ordinary, sinful people to follow Him and be His disciples. In Baptism, You have chosen us to be Your children. We thank you for the great mercy You have shown to us and ask that You would continue to raise up men in the Church who will catch people for Your Kingdom. In Jesus' name we pray. Amen." After the prayer, sing or say the hymn(s) together. Then read the Bible lesson, review introductory material, and read the opening section together.

God Speaks

1. Matthew 4:18–22, which is almost identical to Mark 1:16–20, records a different event than Luke 5:1–11. In Matthew, Jesus is walking along the Sea of Galilee (Gennesaret) and sees Peter and Andrew fishing. Then He tells them, "Follow Me, and I will make you fishers of men" (Matthew 4:19). He also calls James and John, who were mending their nets. On the other hand, Luke says that Jesus was preaching by the shore, and the fishermen were washing their nets, not fishing. Then Jesus gets in Peter's boat, teaches from the boat, and gives Peter a miraculous catch of fish. Only after this does Jesus say to Peter, "From now on you will be catching men" (Luke 5:10).

It seems that Matthew records an event that occurred earlier in Jesus' ministry. Jesus had called Peter, Andrew, James, and John to be His disciples. He had told them to follow Him and He would make them fishers of men. But "I will make you fishers of men" refers to a process that is yet to be completed. In other words, Jesus still needed to bring them to the point when they could fish for men. It is a promise of something that will happen in the future. In Luke 5:10, Jesus says to Peter, "From now on you will be catching men," which means, "From this point forward you will be doing this." In Matthew, Jesus' call to Peter is somewhat indefinite timing-wise. In Luke, the call to Peter is immediate and focused on from this point forward.

2. This section of the Bible study is called "God Speaks," and there is nothing more appropriate for such a section than to discuss what the Word of God is. In Luke 8:21, Jesus tells us that His true family is made up of people who hear

138

His Word and put it into practice. In Luke 11:28, He says that those who hear the Word of God and keep it—that is, believe it—are blessed. These words naturally still apply to the Church. Luther says in the Smalcald Articles (XII 2) that the Church is made up of "holy believers and lambs who hear the voice of their Shepherd." We gather frequently to hear the voice of our Good Shepherd, and we should be encouraged by such passages to continue to do so. As Paul says in Romans 10:17, "Faith comes from hearing, and hearing through the word of Christ."

3. Isaiah saw the Lord upon His throne in His glory. This absolutely terrified him, for he recognized his sinfulness in the presence of a holy God. Yet the Lord sends one of the Seraphim to Isaiah with a burning coal that would forgive his sins and allow him to stand in God's presence without fear. Similarly, while Peter is gripped with terror over his sinfulness, Jesus tells him to not be afraid. This absolution gave him the confidence to stand before the holy Jesus as a forgiven sinner. These stories teach us Law and Gospel. They tell us that the holy God cannot tolerate sin in His presence, but that He is ready to forgive the repentant sinner. The Son of God became incarnate not to condemn sinners but to save them. Though we are poor, miserable sinners and cannot bear the holiness of His presence, the Lord is always ready to absolve us too.

4. Peter stands with the other eleven apostles and throws out the net by proclaiming God's Word. He drags people into the Church through Holy Baptism. They are kept alive by the "apostles' teaching and fellowship" and "the breaking of bread and the prayers" (Acts 2:42). In other words, they continue to thrive on the preached Word of Jesus and feast on His true body and blood in the Lord's Supper, which is also known as the breaking of the bread. This fishing trip continues today as the Church sends out men to bring people in through the Word and Sacraments. We all can take part in this mission by telling our friends and family about Jesus when we have the opportunity. We also can pray that many more people will become men caught alive through the life-giving waters of Holy Baptism.

5. God always speaks to us in Law and Gospel, and this parable contains both. The reality is that unbelievers will be gathered into the Church on earth along with believers. On the Last Day, the fish will be separated out into the good and the bad—the alive and dead—and many will be thrown into hell for eternal judgment. The living fish who have been brought to repentance and faith through God's Word will be received into heaven.

We Live

1. For one thing, hooks often do a lot of damage to the fish. But even more comforting is the fact that the image of a net prevents us from thinking that we somehow brought ourselves into the Church by going for the bait, or that we have to hang on with our own strength. In Baptism, we are reborn. Just as we didn't choose to be born in the first place, nor did we bring our birth about, so are we made members of the Church without our own efforts.

2. Jesus builds the Church. He does it all. Certainly, He uses people to throw out the nets and haul the fish in, but it is comforting to know that not a single fish that Jesus chooses will be lost. Although we may be tempted to despair because the Church does not seem to be growing as rapidly as we would like, remember this story. The catch is the Lord's, not ours.

3. Obviously, not everyone is a trained fisherman. How many other jobs in the world would not be filled if everyone decided to be a fisherman? Each person has various gifts to be used in various vocations. All vocations are pleasing to God when they are done in faith. Jesus uses sinners like us as mothers, fathers, grandparents, students, and workers. Whether you are a butcher, a baker, a candlestick maker, a fisherman, or serve in any other role, you are actually doing the Lord's work by helping your neighbor.

Jesus has promised to raise up men in the Church to catch men alive. Not everyone is called to be a pastor, just as not everyone is called to be a fisherman. The Lord willed that only certain men be called into the Office of the Holy Ministry (1 Timothy 2:12; 3:2). Being a pastor is not a holier calling than any other vocation, but it is a uniquely instituted Office in the Church. While only a few are uniquely called to be full-time fishers of men, all Christians should feel free to share the Gospel when they have the opportunity, but it should always be done out of thanksgiving, not obligation.

Closing

Encourage the adults with children in Sunday School to review their child's Growing in Christ Leaflet together at home.

Lesson 11

The Beatitudes
Matthew 5:1–12

Opening

Open class with a prayer tied to the **Key Point** for the lesson. For example, this week's prayer could be: "Heavenly Father, Your Son, Jesus, explains in the Beatitudes that He was poor, hungry, sorrowful, hated, and rejected for our sake so that You could grant us the gifts and blessings He earned. In Baptism, His righteousness is credited to our account, and our sins are taken away by Him. Please preserve us in faith and teach us to seek our righteousness in Him alone. In Jesus' name we pray. Amen." After the prayer, sing or say the hymn(s) together. Then read the Bible lesson, review the introductory material, and begin the opening questions.

1. A saint is a holy one, and Christ is truly the "Holy One of God." The Beatitudes define much of Jesus' ministry to make us saints. As long as the Christian remains on earth, he is simultaneously sinner and saint. Insofar as he is a sinner, he will fail to live up to the standards of the Beatitudes. Insofar as he is a saint, Christ's saving work is credited to him, and when God looks at him, He sees Christ's fulfillment of the Beatitudes.

2. In Matthew's Gospel, blessedness refers to the status of a person whom God has looked upon graciously and to whom He has given His approval. Unlike the world, which sees blessedness as a reward or as an effect of some meritorious cause, Jesus teaches that blessedness is a gift from God. Blessedness is dependent on the mercy of Christ. In Matthew 16:16–17, Peter makes the great confession that Jesus is the Christ, but Jesus immediately tells him that the Father had revealed that confession to him. Therefore, God was the One who blessed Peter with the opportunity to confess Jesus, and He is the only source of our blessedness.

God Speaks

1. Jesus, out of sheer grace toward us, humbled Himself even to the point of becoming a slave to His disciples. He gave Himself as a ransom in order to provide us with countless blessings. He gave up His Spirit on the cross to richly deliver forgiveness to us.

2. Jesus mourned for Jerusalem and Israel when they did not repent, but He rejoiced after the resurrection as He instituted the Church, the true Israel. He also mourned for us, carrying our grief and sorrows. The Holy Spirit helped Jesus do His work of comforting the mourners. On the Last Day, Jesus will end all mourning for His faithful.

3. When a person is brought into Christ, he is made a new creation, an heir of the new heavens and earth that Christ has prepared through His saving work. At the Last Day, the blessed ones will by grace receive the Kingdom prepared for them since the foundation of the world.

4. When God raised His Son, Jesus, from the dead, He justified—declared Him righteous—to all the world. Since Jesus had taken upon Himself the sin of the world, He had to die to pay the debt owed to God for those sins. Jesus died an unrighteous death because He bore our sin. God declared Jesus righteous when He raised Him from the dead, and in doing so, also declared us righteous.

5. Mercy is a divine attitude toward sinners that pardons debts. Jesus has canceled the debt that we owe for the guilt of our sins through His blood. Mistakenly, many believe that we should pray for God to be patient with us until we renovate our lives, but actually, we need the Lord's undeserved pity, which releases us from our sins and forgives our debts.

6. The blood of Jesus purifies us from all sin. When, in faith, we see the face of Jesus in His Word and Sacraments, we truly see God.

7. Paul says that we have peace with God when we are justified by faith and that we have been reconciled to God through the blood of Jesus' cross. In Baptism, just like Jesus, we are called sons of God, heirs of the Kingdom.

8. Pilate's wife calls Jesus a righteous man, that is, blameless and undeserving of persecution. Barabbas should have been executed, for he was truly unrighteous. We, too, should have died for our unrighteousness, but Jesus suffered for our sins instead, bringing us to God and making us righteous. As He suffered, He remained like a lamb to the slaughter meekly bearing our punishment.

We Live

1. We normally describe blessings as things that we recognize as good gifts from God: a happy family, a good church, wisdom, strength, good health, material possessions. On the other hand, persecution is viewed negatively, since it brings about pain, suffering, doubts, inconvenience, disappointment, and fear.

Jesus rearranges the way we are to view the world. The follower of Jesus is called blessed when he is persecuted for Jesus' sake. Though persecution is not an obvious reason for joy, that is precisely where rejoicing is said to come from. As is so often the case in Holy Scripture, God flips around how the world views life. The false glory for the Church is one of unbridled success; the true cross of the Church is to suffer persecution, just as Christ has.

The apostles in Acts 5 were beaten by the authorities for preaching in Jesus' name. They rejoiced "that they were counted worthy to suffer dishonor for [His] name" (5:41). Instead of taking persecution as a sign to give up, they preached Christ even more vigorously. We should note in this example that the apostles were being persecuted since they were public ministers of the Gospel. Jesus says *when* they revile or persecute you," not *if*. Persecution for the faith is a sign of faith, but the absence of persecution at a specific time in a Christian's life does not equate to an absence of faith. We can rejoice in persecution for Jesus' sake, since He is blessing us with the opportunity to confess His name and participate in His sufferings (1 Peter 4:13). However, we also should rejoice in the times of peace that the Lord gives us. The key to it all is faith. If we believe that we are the Lord's in good times and bad and are willing to confess His name even at the risk of persecution, then we can remain confident and content no matter the situation.

Closing

Encourage the adults with children in Sunday School to review their child's Growing in Christ Leaflet together at home.

Also encourage the study of the catechism together.

Lesson 12

The Transfiguration
Luke 9:28–36

Opening

Open class with a prayer tied to the **Key Point** for the lesson. For example, this week's prayer could be: "Heavenly Father, on the Mount of Transfiguration, You showed that Your Son, Jesus, is the fulfillment of the Law and the Prophets, and You declared that we should listen to Him, our Savior. Grant us ears of faith, that we might hear His Word and daily grow in our faith. In Jesus' name we pray. Amen." After the prayer, sing or say the hymn(s) together. Then read the Bible lesson, review introductory material, and begin the opening questions.

1. Isaiah 53 foretells that the Messiah (Christ) would suffer for the sins of the people and describes how He would suffer. Of course, many people thought that the Christ would be a powerful earthly ruler and did not expect that He would be enthroned weakly on a cross. It took a lot of time for Jesus' disciples to grasp this concept. Even though He told them explicitly that He would suffer, die, and rise again, they did not get it. They, too, thought in glory terms. As God's children, we live a life under the cross, our lives afflicted with the results of sin—ours and sin in the world. Our Savior who suffered for us is with us in our sufferings through our Baptism. When we are finally called to heaven, we will then live in glory. Now we see dimly, there we shall see Him face-to-face in all His glory.

In Luke 9:23–27, the well-known teaching of Jesus is communicated that His followers are to take up their crosses. We know that the cross is an instrument of pain and death, so these verses are a reminder that, as Paul and Barnabas taught in Acts 14:22, "through many tribulations we must enter the kingdom of God." This does not mean that bearing the cross is a good work that merits salvation. Rather, the Christian receives hardship, frustration, pain, and persecution in his life—all things that challenge his faith—and bearing the cross means that in the midst of these sufferings, the Christian continues to believe in Christ's forgiveness and mercy and does not conclude that God has forsaken him. Just as Christ's life involved suffering before glory, our life will be shaped by that pattern as well.

God Speaks

1. In Exodus 34, Moses' face radiated with the glory from being in the presence of God on Mount Sinai. When he came down from the mountain, he spoke the Word of God to Israel. In Exodus 24, the cloud that covered the mountain represented the glory and presence of the Lord. The cloud at the transfiguration indicates that the glory and presence of God is located in Jesus. He is the "sunrise from on high," who gives "light to those who sit in darkness and the shadow of death" and guides "our feet into the way of peace" through the forgiveness of sins (Luke 1:76–79).

2. In Luke 9:36, the fact that "Jesus was found alone" emphatically indicates that Moses and Elijah no longer take precedence. Moses and Elijah often represent the Law and the Prophets, and because of the context, Jesus remaining alone indicates that He has superseded them. In John 1, Jesus is described as the only Son of the Father who revealed the Father's glory, and that John and other witnesses have seen His glory. This could be a reference to the transfiguration, along with the crucifixion and resurrection. John goes on to contrast Jesus with Moses. Though the Law was important—and was a gift from God—Jesus is greater, for He has revealed the Father's grace and truth in a way that Moses never could have. Jesus is the incarnate Son, full of grace and truth.

3. Psalm 78 records a large portion of the salvation history of Israel. Verses 51–55 recount the Lord's gracious leading of His people out of Egypt, saving them from slavery and defeating their enemies. He then gave them the Promised Land. Essentially, God saved them, provided for them, and mercifully forgave their sins. The exodus is the paradigmatic salvation event in the history of Israel—until Jesus arrived, of course! The exodus was preached on and the people were to recall it as a trustworthy foundation for God's promises to them. Jesus' own exodus followed the pattern of the Old Testament one, since the Father proved Himself trustworthy for our salvation by raising His Son from the dead. We recall that Jesus' promised His continuing presence with His people, the Church, just as the Lord had done for His Old Testament people.

4. In the transfiguration, Jesus appears alongside two other men; He does the same on the cross, and the contrast is striking—glory versus darkness. In the transfiguration, Jesus' garments shone like the sun; on the cross, He is naked, and they cast lots for His garments. In the transfiguration, His glory as the Son

of God is shown; on the cross, He is mocked with shame but also reveals His glory as the Suffering Servant, the true King of the Jews. In the transfiguration, Jesus is hailed by the Father as "My Chosen One"; on the cross, the crowds mockingly say that, if He were really "the Chosen One," He would come down from the cross and save Himself. These are further examples that the intention of the transfiguration is to point us toward the crucifixion and help the reader learn the theology of the cross.

5. We have seen that Moses and Elijah represent the Law and the Prophets. Moses and the Prophets are mentioned in Luke 24:44 and also in 24:27 as those who prophesied that the Christ would die and rise from the dead on the third day. In this, we find the key to reading the Bible—both Old and New Testaments. We are to find Jesus in all the Scriptures. He is the key.

We Live

1. From our lesson, we can say that the saints and angels in heaven talk about Jesus. Moses and Elijah come from heaven not just to look at Jesus or worship Him but to talk about His exodus. Just as Moses led God's people out of sin and death in Egypt, so Jesus leads His people out of sin and death by being the Passover Lamb who will be slaughtered for their sins. He was the firstborn Son whom God did not pass over, but upon whom He poured out all of His wrath against sinners.

Moses, Elijah, and all the saints of heaven talk about what we get to read and hear about this upcoming Lent and Easter season: the suffering, death, resurrection, and ascension of Jesus. Although all of this happened on earth, those in heaven are very interested in it because it accomplished their salvation too. The Gospel of salvation in Jesus is the most wonderful, great, and eternal topic of conversation in heaven. How much more eagerly can the Church share this Gospel with each other and those who have never heard of this Good News in Christ.

2. In Luke 3:21, Jesus is praying after His Baptism and the Father reveals Him as His Son. In Luke 9:18, Jesus is praying right before He asks the disciples, "Who do you say that I am?" and Peter reveals Him as "the Christ of God" (Luke 9:20). In Luke 9:28, Jesus is praying when His transfiguration occurs. Since we find Jesus praying at these significant events, it highlights the importance of each of them in Jesus' ministry. Further, it underscores the importance of prayer in Jesus'—and the Christian's—life. Jesus relied on His Father completely and frequently came to Him in prayer. We have the privilege also to come to Him at any time.

3. The children of Israel long expected the prophet like Moses who would come and speak God's Word to them. The Lord had promised to raise this prophet up one day, and the transfiguration reveals Jesus as that prophet, in fact, He is the very Word Incarnate. He is the one who actually sent the Holy Spirit to inspire the prophet Moses to write about Him in the first place. He also gave the Holy Spirit to the apostles, such as Peter, as an eyewitness to Jesus' majestic transfiguration. Peter says that the prophetic Word—the Scriptures—that the Lord has inspired for our use are actually surer witnesses than eyes could ever have been. In recording the Word of God, "men spoke from God as they were carried along by the Holy Spirit," (2 Peter 1:21) so that we can continue always to listen to Jesus. This is why we go to church too. The preached Word of Christ has great power, and He is the only way to the Father.

Closing

Encourage the adults with children in Sunday School to review their child's Growing in Christ Leaflet together at home.

Lesson 13

The Temptation of Jesus
Luke 4:1–13

Opening

Open class with a prayer tied to the **Key Point** for the lesson. For example, this week's prayer could be: "Lord God, You allowed Jesus to be tempted in the wilderness by Satan, and by remaining faithful to Your Word, He overcame all temptation because we could not. Thank you for crediting His righteousness to our account. As we begin the Lenten season, in which we meditate on Jesus' saving work for us, preserve us from Satan's temptations to despair of Your mercy. In Jesus' name we pray. Amen." After the prayer, sing or say the hymn(s) together. Then read the Bible lesson, review introductory material, and begin the opening questions.

1. Even if we can avoid succumbing to a specific temptation, our minds usually imagine what it would be like to give in to the temptation. Such thoughts are often lustful or cause us to doubt God's Word. Jesus resisted both sinful thoughts and actions in His temptation.

2. As we read about the temptation of Jesus, we are tempted to say, "It was easy for Him since He is true God and has power over Satan" or "It wasn't a real temptation since He couldn't possibly have sinned." It is certainly impossible for our reason to understand how Jesus truly encountered temptation, but God's Word tells us that He was tempted in every way, just as we are, but He was without sin. And it is an important truth, since Jesus' experience of temptation was like ours—painful! It was part of His suffering on our behalf.

3. There is a strong temptation to conclude that the main point of the temptation of Jesus is to provide us with a three-step method for resisting temptation. While we are right to imitate Christ's use of God's Word when we face temptation, as sinners, we fail to trust God's Word perfectly. As we will see, the main point is that Jesus' resistance of Satan is on our behalf—doing what we could not do for our salvation!

God Speaks

1. Jesus was baptized in order to set in motion His task of fulfilling all righteousness. He placed Himself under sinners' Baptism in order to experience all the things they do, except He did not sin. Throughout His life,

148

He would actively obey God's Law and fulfill it perfectly. He never wavered in His trust for His Father. He lived as the perfect man. So when we are baptized into Christ, His active obedience of the Law is credited to us, since we cannot. Likewise, Jesus' passive obedience on the cross won forgiveness for the debt of our sins, which we could not pay. Jesus' active obedience earned us righteousness; His passive obedience earned us the forgiveness of sins. In Jesus, we have eternal life.

2. "Did God really say . . . ?" This is Satan's favorite line. Eve added "you must not touch it" to the command from God. Whenever we add or subtract from God's Word, we are in for trouble. In Exodus 17, Israel tempted God by not believing that He would take care of them in the wilderness. They asked, "Is the Lord among us or not?" In response, God patiently provided a miracle for them, giving them water from a rock. Massah means "testing" and Meribah means "quarrelling," both providing reminders of Israel's faithlessness in the wilderness.

3. Satan comes to the Son of God and says, "You're no Son of God. If you were, you would make this stone into bread." The devil challenges Jesus to despair God's love for Him, saying, "If He loved You, He would have fed You! Besides, if You are really the Son, You could make bread and prove Your Sonship." But Jesus knows His Father's trustworthiness. In Deuteronomy 8, Moses tells Israel to remember how the Lord was with them for the forty years in the wilderness providing manna. Jesus could be confident that His Father would provide for Him. Yet we also see that when God tested Israel's faithfulness, they failed miserably. But Jesus does not. He knows that the Word of God is all that He needs to live by.

4. Satan offers Jesus the power and glory of Easter without the pain and suffering of Good Friday. We can never forget the true stress and strain Jesus experienced for us as He marched steadily toward the cross. He prayed that, if possible, the Father could save the world in another way. But even as He sweated out drops of blood, He again showed His perfect obedience to the Father's will through His faithful prayer. When Jesus responded to Satan, He quoted from Deuteronomy 6 that the Lord, who had brought Israel out of slavery in Egypt, was worthy of exclusive trust. Satan was another god to be resisted. Though Israel had continually chased after other gods, Jesus remained true to the Lord God.

5. Israel faithlessly tested God in the wilderness by doubting God's presence. Jesus resists this temptation to prove God. He does not need any other sign

than what He received in His Baptism. The Word of God called Him the Son of God, and an external sign was unnecessary. Yet even after resisting this temptation, Jesus would continue to face Satan throughout His ministry, as the devil sought many opportune times to subvert Jesus from His Father's will to save us.

We Live

1. To despair means to conclude that God does not love you, that you have no hope of being saved, and that your life is worthless. You feel alone, abandoned, and forsaken by God. This is how Satan tries to tempt the starving Son of God. Despair is a deadly sin. Though God is love, despair calls Him unloving. Though God's mercy endures forever, despair calls Him unmerciful. But Jesus did not despair. He stayed the course in order to save us. This is our weapon against despair: Jesus Christ, in whom our sins are forgiven. Nothing, not even Satan, can harm us!

2. People are tempted to divorce by thoughts such as "The Lord wants me to be happy" or "It would be better for the children" or "It's better than fighting all the time." People are tempted toward abortion by "The world doesn't need one more unwanted baby" or "We're too young to raise a baby" or "The child would suffer terribly with its deformity." We look at outcomes that appear good and are tempted to sin. Satan rarely tempts us with obviously evil things. More often, he uses apparently good things. The suffering and cross of Jesus appears evil, but Jesus knows that this is the only way to the highest good, our salvation. He loves us and will not skip over the cross to receive glory for Himself. Jesus rejects Satan's temptations toward apparently good things by embracing God's good Word and going to the apparently evil cross for us.

3. You hear people argue that "The Bible says to forgive others," so criminals should not be punished severely. "The Bible says not to judge others," so that means it is wrong to judge homosexuality as a sin. "The Bible says that God is love," and it would be unloving to tell someone that living together outside of marriage is sinful. The devil loves to take the Word of God and make it mean something that it does not. God's Word is not a waxen nose that we can twist to fit our agenda. Jesus shows us that the Word is solid, when He responds with "It is said," not just, "It is written." Jesus corrects the devil's interpretation and tells him what it really means. What the Bible says about the angels' protection cannot mean that you should recklessly throw yourself into their arms because the Bible also says, "Do not put God to the test."

4. After His Baptism, Jesus is immediately taken into the wilderness by the Spirit to face temptation by Satan. Likewise, after receiving Baptism, the Christian immediately begins to be attacked by Satan, who roams about looking for people to devour. He desires nothing more than to rip Christians from God's hands. But Jesus Christ defends us from the devil's attacks. Through His Word of forgiveness and through Baptism, Absolution, and the Lord's Supper, the Lord strengthens our faith and fights against Satan for us. For His divine protection, we flee to receive His saving gifts at church!

Closing

Encourage the adults with children in Sunday School to review their child's Growing in Christ Leaflet together at home.